The Twelfth

Ada Leverson

Alpha Editions

This edition published in 2024

ISBN : 9789362517005

Design and Setting By
Alpha Editions
www.alphaedis.com
Email - info@alphaedis.com

As per information held with us this book is in Public Domain.
This book is a reproduction of an important historical work. Alpha Editions uses the best technology to reproduce historical work in the same manner it was first published to preserve its original nature. Any marks or number seen are left intentionally to preserve its true form.

Contents

CHAPTER I ....- 1 -
CHAPTER II ....- 10 -
CHAPTER III ....- 15 -
CHAPTER IV ....- 19 -
CHAPTER V ....- 27 -
CHAPTER VI ....- 35 -
CHAPTER VII ....- 41 -
CHAPTER VIII ....- 50 -
CHAPTER IX ....- 57 -
CHAPTER X ....- 64 -
CHAPTER XI ....- 71 -
CHAPTER XII ....- 76 -
CHAPTER XIII ....- 80 -
CHAPTER XIV ....- 86 -
CHAPTER XV ....- 91 -
CHAPTER XVI ....- 98 -
CHAPTER XVII ....- 101 -
CHAPTER XVIII ....- 105 -
CHAPTER XIX ....- 113 -
CHAPTER XX ....- 122 -
CHAPTER XXI ....- 130 -
CHAPTER XXII ....- 136 -
CHAPTER XXIII ....- 139 -
CHAPTER XXIV ....- 143 -
CHAPTER XXV ....- 147 -
CHAPTER XXVI ....- 152 -

CHAPTER XXVII ....- 158 -
CHAPTER XXVIII ....- 164 -

CHAPTER I

FELICITY

"Hallo, Greenstock! Lady Chetwode in?"

"Her ladyship is not at home, sir. But she is sure to see you, Master Savile," said the butler, with a sudden and depressing change of manner, from correct impassibility to the conventional familiarity of a patronising old retainer.

"Dressing, eh? You look all right Greenstock."

"Well, I am well, and I am not well, Master Savile, if you can understand that, sir. My harsthma" (so he pronounced it), "'as been exceedingly troublesome lately."

"Ah, that's capital!" Not listening, the boy—he was sixteen, dark, and very handsome, with a determined expression, and generally with an air of more self-control than seemed required for the occasion—walked up deliberately, three steps at a time, knocked, with emphasis, at his sister's dressing-room door, and said—

"I say, Felicity, can I come in?"

"Who's there? Don't come in!"

Upon which invitation he entered the room with a firm step.

"Oh, it's you, Savile darling. I am glad to see you! Dear pet! Come and tell me all about everything—papa and the party—and, look out, dear, don't tread on my dresses! Give Mr. Crofton a chair, Everett. Even you mustn't sit down on a perfectly new hat!"

Felicity was a lovely little blonde creature about twenty-five years old, dressed in a floating Watteau-like garment of vaporous blue, painted with faded pink roses. She was seated in a large carved and gilded chair, opposite an excessively Louis-Quinze mirror, while her pale golden hair was being brushed out by a brown, inanimate-looking maid. Her little oval face, with its soft cloudy hair growing low on the forehead, long blue eyes, and rosebud mouth, had something of the romantic improbability of an eighteenth-century miniature. From the age of two Felicity had been an acknowledged beauty. She profited by her grasp of this fact merely by being more frank than most charming people, and more natural than most disagreeable ones. With little self-consciousness, she took a cool sportsmanlike pleasure in the effect she produced, and perhaps enjoyed the envy and admiration she had excited in her perambulator in Kensington Gardens almost as much as her most showy successes in later life.

The most effective of these (so far) had been her marriage. Hopelessly bowled over, as he called it, by her detailed loveliness, and not even frightened by her general brilliance, Lord Chetwode had insisted on her making the match of the previous season. He was a good-looking, amiable, and wealthy young man, who was as lavish as if he had not had a penny, and who showed his extravagantly long descent chiefly by being (for a racing man) rather eccentrically interested in the subject of decoration.

He was an owner of racehorses and a collector of curiosities, and these tastes gave him certain interests apart from his wife. He was, however, very much in love with her, and showed it chiefly by writing her nearly every day long, elaborate, and conspicuously illegible love-letters. She was not an expert in handwriting, nor had she time or patience to decipher them. So she merely treasured them (unread) in a green and white striped silk box. For under all her outward sentimentality, Felicity was full of tenderness, especially for her husband. This was not surprising, for he was a most agreeable companion, a great friend, quite devoted to her, to his pretty home in London, and his picturesque old house in the country, from all of which, however, he was as a rule markedly absent. If one asked after Chetwode, the answer was nearly always that he was away.

He had chosen every detail of the house in Park Street with a patience worthy of his passion. In the bedroom, especially, not a concession was made, not a point stretched. All was purest Louis-Quinze. But in spite of this, and amidst all her tapestry and old French furniture, Felicity had a very contemporary air. About everything was the recent look characteristic of the home of a lately married couple. The room looked as if it had been decorated the day before for a twentieth-century Madame de Pompadour. But, if the background was almost archæological, the atmosphere was absolutely modern. In this incongruity was a certain fascination.

Though the bridal freshness still lingered, a more wilful element was also observable. Invitation-cards, race-cards, the *Daily Mail*, magazines, English and French novels, and cigarettes were freely scattered about, and an expert would have seen at a glance that the dresses lying in every direction could not have formed part of any trousseau. They had obviously been chosen with (or against) the advice of Lord Chetwode.

Savile sat down on a pink curved sofa, and said definitely—

"Look here, Felicity, I want to speak to you."

"Yes, darling?"

"Does Chetwode know what's going to win the Cambridgeshire?"

"How can he know, darling? Would it be fair? Of course he has some vague *idea*. Candid Friend he said was the favourite. He says it's a certainty. But *his* certainties! (Everett, look out. You've been overdoing the waving lately. Remember how careful I have to be not to look like a wax-doll in a hairdresser's shop ... with *my* complexion)! Go on, Savile,—what's the party going to be like?"

"Like nothing on earth, my dear, as usual. One of the governor's baffling entertainments."

"Well, I don't care what people say, Savile! I think papa's parties are the greatest fun one can get anywhere. It's a wonderful mixture,—a sort of Russian salad. How exciting it is, for instance, never being quite sure whether one is going to be taken to dinner by—Lord Rosebery, or—Little Tich!"

"As it happens, my dear, they've both refused," said Savile ironically.

"Oh, Savile, don't be funny when I've no time to laugh. Do you deny papa's peculiar talent for celebrities? Is De Valdez coming?"

"The Spanish composer? Oh, rather! He's coming over about his new opera. He's all right. At least, I bear him rather, but girls like him."

"And who will be the great card this time, Savile?"

"Of course, Roy Beaumont, the inventor."

"What on earth's he invented?"

"Himself, I should think. He's only about twenty-one. Roy's a capital chap, really. The only thing is, he wears hats that he thinks suit him. Otherwise he dresses rather well, for a dandy."

"Why on earth shouldn't his hats suit him?" said Lady Chetwode in surprise.

"Oh, never mind! I can't go into all that. Why, because you ought to wear things, because they're *right*, not because——Oh, girls don't understand dress! Don't let's fatigue ourselves discussing it. Any one can see you've never been to Eton."

"Well, I should rather hope they could," murmured Felicity, looking in the glass.

"F. J. Rivers and Arthur Mervyn, the actor, are coming, and—oh, a lot more."

"I see, it's a clever party. Isn't it fun, Savile, being the only stupid person in a crowd of clever people? They make such a fuss about one. Aren't any real people coming?"

"A few. Some heavy M.P.'s and their wives, and Aunt William, and of course old Ridokanaki."

"Oh, the Greek millionaire,—the banker?"

"Don't call him the banker; it reminds me of *The Hunting of the Snark*."

Felicity laughed.

"Yes; Mr. Ridokanaki is rather like a sort of Snark, and you and papa are hunting him for Sylvia. Will it come off?"

"Shouldn't think so," said Savile thoughtfully. "He's rather a bore, but he's a good sort. Of course, Sylvia ought to marry him. All the pretty girls are marrying these Anglo-Aliens. He's very keen. But about my affairs—I say, Everett, do take away these fluffy rustling things."

Everett having completed her task, with a stiff smile, and a rainbow of chiffons over her arm, faded away.

Felicity, completely dressed, turned her chair round and put up her absurd little high-heeled shoes.

"Now then, fire away, old boy."

Savile, taking this command literally, stretched out his hand for the cigarettes. Felicity snatched them away.

"How dare you! You won't grow any more! Here, have a chocolate!"

Savile looked at her with a pitying smile and said slowly—

"What rot! Grow! As if I wanted to grow! As if I had the time! I've got more serious things than that to do I can tell you. I have two rather awful troubles. Look here. Things are a bit off at home just now. The Governor is furious about Chetwode not coming to the party."

Lady Chetwode's colour deepened.

"Well, what about me, Savile? Do you think I'm pleased? Is it my fault the Cambridgeshire's run on Wednesday? Do be just to me! Do I make the racing engagements? You can't pretend that I can alter the rules of Newmarket because papa chooses to give a lot of absurd parties!"

"I know, old girl—but can't you make him give it up?"

"Who ever yet made Chetwode give up anything he wants to do? Besides, it's not like a dinner-party, or his wedding, or anything like that, Savile, you know. After all, he isn't *bound* to be there!"

"All right; only it's the first thing we've given since your marriage and——"

"I know, dear. I'm very angry about it. Very. Besides, I'm sure I don't care if the darling prefers racing! Don't you know by this time that whenever

Chetwode is particularly wanted he is sure to be either at Kempton or at Christie's?"

"Spending at Christie's what he's lost at Kempton, I suppose."

"Naturally, Savile. And if he prefers his horses, and his jockeys, and his bookmakers, and even his old furniture, to taking his own wife to her own father's party——"

"Hallo, old girl, don't tell me you haven't everything under the sun you want! Because that would be a bit too thick," said Savile, sitting up.

"Who says I haven't?"

"No one, if you don't."

"I should hope not!"

Then Felicity murmured relentingly—

"Dear Chetwode! He's so heavenly in some ways. No, I won't worry and oppose him, it's a fatal mistake. We'll make it up to you later—stay with you on the river in August or something. What price you, dear? What's your trouble?"

Savile fumbled a good deal with a tassel, laughed mirthlessly, frowned gloomily, and then said with a jerk: "What price me? No price. It's her. You know."

Felicity replied patiently.

"You always say that, and you never get any further,—never."

"Well, my dear, don't you see—there's two things."

"Go on."

"What ought a chap to do who,—I've consulted men of the world, and yet I think you know best. You're so celebrated as a confidante."

"Well?" said his sister.

"What ought a chap to do—who ... oh, well ... if a chap—say a chap has—well—a girl, say, frightfully keen on him (for the sake of the argument), and she's a decent sort of girl, and at the same time the poor chap is frightfully keen on another girl, who is frightfully keen on another chap—who is a very decent chap too, mind you ... what ought he to do?"

"Which chap, Savile?"

"Oh, don't be so muddle-headed, Felicity! Pull yourself together, can't you? *Me*, of course!"

"Oh, you!"

"Yes."

"You mean Dolly Clive is in love with you" (Savile winced at the feminine explicitness), "and you are in love with some one else, and it's quite hopeless."

"I don't quite say that. But there are tremendous difficulties."

"Is she married? Oh, I do believe she's married. Oh, Savile! How extraordinary and horrid of you!"

"Oh, it's all right, Felicity," said Savile, with a reassuring nod, at which she laughed.

"I'm sure it is, dear. But who on earth is it?"

Savile took a photograph out of his pocket, and blushingly showed it to his sister, with his head turned away.

As she looked at it her face expressed the most unfeigned bewilderment.

"Aunt William? But this is very sudden.... Oh, it's some mistake, surely! You *can't* be in love with Aunt William!"

With a howl of fury Savile snatched the portrait from her.

It was a quaint, faded photograph of an elderly aunt of his taken in the early seventies. It represented a woman with an amiable expression and a pointed face; parted hair, with a roll on the top, and what was in those days known as an Alexandra curl on the left shoulder. She was leaning her head on her hand, and her elbow on a vague shelf or balcony. The photograph was oval in shape, and looked as if the lady were looking out of a window. At the base of the window was a kind of board, on which was written in her own handwriting, magnified (in white letters, relieved on black), the beautiful words, "Yours truly, Mary Crofton."

"You are an idiot, Felicity!" said Savile angrily. "You make fun of everything! I gave it you by mistake. I took it from Aunt William's album for a joke. Give it me."

"Don't snatch! I want another prehistoric peep—and now tell me the real person, dear," said Felicity, trying not to laugh.

"Oh no, you don't! I just shan't now."

"Mayn't I see the real one?"

Savile, after a glance at Aunt William, gave a short laugh, and said, putting it away—

"Look here, and try to listen. This is how I stand. Last holidays, at Christmas, I proposed to Dolly Clive in the square. She accepted me. Very well. This holidays, I saw some one else; what is a fellow to do? And then I went completely off my head about her, as any chap with a grain of sense would do, and Doll's no more to me now than———"

"Aunt William," said Lady Chetwode.

"As a gentleman, I'm bound to Dolly; though, *don't* forget I always told her that if when she came out she met a chap she liked better, she was quite free; (not but what I jolly well intended to punch the chap's head). Still, there it was! Then this happens! And this time I fell really in love."

"Where?"

"Never mind where. At a concert."

"But what concert, Savile?"

"*A* concert."

"Whose concert? You've only been to one in your life. I know———the Albert Hall!"

"You've hit in once, my dear."

"Is it?"

"Yes. Adelina Patti."

Savile got up and looked out of the window.

Felicity looked serious. Then she said gaily—

"Poor old boy! I think, dear, you should try and forget it."

"I can't, Felicity! She haunts me! Oh, the way she sings 'Comin through the Rye!' She's simply—well, ripping's the only word!"

"It's hereditary. You're just like papa. He was madly in love with her once."

"Only once!" Savile was contemptuous.

"Well, Savile dear, anyhow I advise you to break it off definitely with Dolly. She's only just fourteen now, and it would interfere with her lessons. Besides, I know her mother wants her to go in for Physical Culture during the holidays. What are those exercises—Swedenborgian or something—anyhow, it takes up time. Besides, I somehow feel that that (the affair with Dolly) was more a sort of boy-and-girl fancy. Don't you think so? This, of course, is the great romance of your life. It will probably last for ever. Of course I know it's only a kind of distant worship and adoration, but still———"

"How well you know, by Jove! Felicity, I tell you what—I'm not going to think about it any more. I *know* there's no hope. Is she likely to sing again this season?"

"Perhaps."

"Oh, Felicity, let me come with you!... No, I won't. I'd rather go alone in the balcony."

"We'll see, dear. Now, what's the other trouble?"

"Well, I'm rather worried about Sylvia."

"Oh, my dear boy, that's a mania of yours! You're always harping on about her marrying Mr. Ridokanaki."

"Why shouldn't she?"

"Why should she, Savile? It wouldn't amuse her. And Sylvia is very happy at home; the head of papa's house, perfect liberty, and only twenty——"

"I know; but do you know I sometimes suspect ... look here. Do you think Woodville—don't you think Sylvia ... likes him?"

Felicity sat up with a jerk.

"Frank Woodville! That highly-principled, highly-strung, highly-cultivated, intellectual young man? Oh *no*! *Oh* no! Why he, as papa's secretary, would no more try to——"

"Who says he would? She might like him all right, I suppose. Besides, if he *is* highly cultivated, as you call it, and all that, it's not his fault, is it? He's a good-looking chap all the same. Face facts, I say! and if the truth were known, and every one had their rights, he *may* be human! You never know!"

Felicity laughed, and then said—

"I do hope he's not. It would be so impossible! Rather romantic too, a puritanical secretary with a figure and a profile in love with the pretty daughter of a pompous politician. He teaches her Latin too. Sort of Abelard and Francesca—or something—But oh! I don't believe it."

"Abelard! Oh, what rot! Do shut up! Well, remember I've given you a hint, and I don't ask you not to tell—I treat you as an officer and a gentleman."

"Don't worry about me," said Felicity, smiling, "I talk so much that I never have time to repeat a single thing about anybody—to the wrong person."

"I know. Will you dine with us to-morrow, as Chetwode's out of town?"

"No, Savile darling, I can't. I'm dining with Mrs. Ogilvie. You needn't mention it."

Savile arranged his tie in the mirror, and said in his slow, impressive way—

"I don't mention things. But the Governor doesn't care for that go-ahead set. And he's not wrong, either."

"We're only going to dine at Ranelagh,—to try her new motor, dear," said Felicity coaxingly.

"Does Chetwode know?"

"I thought you knew he was at Newmarket."

"Well! Take it as you like, and think me an interfering ass if you choose, but if I were you I'd somehow get Chetwode back from Newmarket,—and not go about so much with Mrs. Ogilvie."

"Why not, Savile?"

"Well, I shouldn't begin that drifting apart business, *just* yet. It's really rather rot, quite so soon. You're too young, and so on—been married a year, and I'm hanged if he's not fond of you still! Why do it? That's what I say——"

"A person may be very devoted, *and* a perfect husband, and sweet in every way, and not dream of drifting apart for ages and ages, and yet want to see Tobacco Trust run, darling!"

"I know,—and I've put my last shilling on Penultimate!"

"Naughty boy! I hope it was really your last shilling,—not your last sovereign!"

He laughed, kissed her, and walked downstairs, softly humming to himself, "Gin a body meet a body...."

When he had gone, Felicity looked quite sensible for a little while as she pondered indulgently on the weaknesses of her husband, cheerfully on the troubles of her brother, and with some real sisterly anxiety concerning the alarming attractions of Frank Woodville.

CHAPTER II

THE TRIALS OF WOODVILLE

Several hours of the morning had been passed by Woodville in an occupation that, one might think, would easily pall on a spirited young man—addressing envelopes and filling in invitation cards. The cards stated with tedious repetition that Miss Crofton and Sir James Crofton, M.P., would be At Home on the 30th April at ten o'clock. In the left-hand corner were the words, "Herr Yung's White Viennese Orchestra."

Woodville's desk was close to the long French window, which opened on to a charming garden. From this garden came the sound of excited twitterings of birds and other pleasant suggestions of spring. Suddenly a tall and graceful young girl, with hair like sunshine, came up to the open window and smiled at him. She held up to show him some wonderful mauve and blue hyacinths that she carried, and then passed on. Woodville sighed. *It* was too symbolic. The scent lingered. Like a half-remembered melody, it seemed to have the insidious power of recalling something in the past that was too wonderful ever to have happened, and of suggesting vague hopes of the most improbable joys. Sylvia seemed to the young man the incarnation of April. He put down his pen, and shaded his eyes with his hand. Then the inner door from the hall opened, and a pompous but genial voice exclaimed with heavy briskness—

"Well, Woodville, finished, eh?"

"Not yet, Sir James, but I can go on later, if you want me now."

The secretary spoke with a deference that seemed surprising. He did not look like a man who would be supple to an employer, or obsequious to any one—even a woman.

"No hurry, no hurry," said Sir James, with that air of self-denial that conveys the urgent necessity of intense speed. He was a handsome old man, with thick grey hair, a white military moustache, bushy dark eyebrows, and in his eyes that humorous twinkle that is so often seen in those men of the last generation who are most devoid of a sense of humour. Sir James was liable to the irritable changes of mood that would nowadays be called neurotic or highly strung, but was in his young days merely put down as bad temper. He had a high estimation of his mental powers, and a poor opinion of those who did not share this estimation. He took a special pride in his insight into character, and in that instinctive penetration that is said to enable its fortunate possessor to see as far through a brick wall as most people. (A modest ambition, when all is said and done!) His contemporaries liked him: at least, they smiled when his name was mentioned. He was warm-hearted and generous; he had a curious mania for celebrities; was a hospitable host, a tedious guest, and a loyal friend. His late wife (who was lovely, but weary) had always described him in one word. The word was "trying".

Sir James sat down slowly on a depressed leather uneasy chair, and said, "Presently I want you to take notes of a speech I intend making in the House on Russia—I mean the present situation in Russia," he added instructively.

"Of course," said Woodville, trying to look intelligently sympathetic, and restraining his inclination to say that he had not expected a speech at this time of day on our victories in the Crimea.

"Do let's have the speech while it's fresh in your mind. I can easily return to this afterwards, Sir James."

"Later on, later on; when it's more matured—more matured...." He pondered a few moments about nothing whatever, and then said, "Sent a card to Roy Beaumont, the young inventor? That's right. That boy has a future. Mark my words, he has a future before him."

"Oh! I thought it had begun some time ago, and was still going on. He is quite twenty-three, isn't he?" asked Frank.

"About that—about that. He's a young man with Ideas, Woodville."

"Yes. I heard he had grown tired of button-holes, and is thinking of training a creeper to crawl up the lapel of his coat."

"An original notion," said Sir James judicially. "If practicable. And what else did he invent?"

"Wasn't it he who invented some new way of not posting letters—by electricity?"

"I rather think you're confusing him with Marconi," said Sir James, shaking his head. "But I always detect genius! It's a curious thing, Woodville, but I never make a mistake! By the way, I should like to send a card to the Leader of the Opposition and his wife. Inquire of Sylvia about their address. I don't know them, socially, but I fancy they would be rather surprised if I omitted them."

"It might, indeed, be rather marked," said Woodville, making a note, and remembering that it is as impossible nowadays to ask every one one knows as to know every one one asks.

"Well, I'll leave you to your work, and we'll do the speech later, a little later ... much later," and Sir James meditatively bent his elbows on the arms of the chair, accurately placed all the tips of his fingers together, and slowly blinked his eyes. He did not mean any harm by this. In fact, he meant nothing. His gestures and expression had no significance at all. He simply behaved like any other elderly Anglo-Saxon who believes himself to be political and to resemble the "Younger Pitt."

"I rather wanted to ask Miss Crofton about a change of address," said Woodville, glancing swiftly and hypocritically through the Red Book.

"I'll send her to you—I'll send her. Don't move. Sit still, sit still."

Woodville followed with his eyes the closing of the door; then he put down his pen and gazed at the closed door. Sometimes he thought his life was like a closed door. Yet, perhaps, there might be some one on the other side of the door? (According to Maeterlinck—or is it Owen Seaman?—there is always some one on the other side of a door.)

At a casual glance Woodville seemed the conventional type of a good-looking young Englishman, tall, fair-haired, and well built. He possessed, however, a forehead unnecessarily intellectual; and a sparkle of more than mere animal spirits lurked in the depths of his dark brown eyes. An observer would also have noticed that his mouth and chin had something of the stern and sad look of fatalism that one sees in the pictures of Rossetti and Burne-Jones. He had the unmistakable public-school and University hall-mark, and if he had been fairly liked at Eton, at Oxford, where (as Mr. Max Beerbohm so rightly says) the nonsense knocked out of one at school is carefully and painlessly put back, Woodville was really popular, and considered remarkably clever, capable of enjoying, and even of conceiving, Ideas. Detesting the ready-made cheap romantic, and yet in vague search of the unusual, he often complained bitterly that his history—so far—was like the little piece of explanation of the plot (for those who have missed it) at the beginning of a chapter of a feuilleton in the *Daily Mail*. It was rather hard to have to admit that he had been left an orphan at three years old and adopted by his bachelor uncle, a baronet called Sir Bryce Woodville, who had brought him up as his acknowledged heir, with the prospect of a big estate.

Frank had gone with careless gaiety through school and college, when his apparently sane and kind relative, growing tired of romantic drama, suddenly behaved like a guardian in an old-fashioned farce. Instead of making his wife his housekeeper, as most men do, he made his housekeeper his wife. She was a depressing woman. In a year he had a son and heir, and within two months after this event, he died, leaving his nephew exactly one hundred pounds a year.

This curiously unpractical joke taught the young man that absurdly improbable things are quite as liable to happen in real life as in weak literature.

The legacy was, of course, abject poverty to a man who, having always had an exceptionally large allowance, had naturally never thought about money, and though Frank believed himself not to be extravagant because he had never made large debts, his ideas of the ordinary necessities of life were not conspicuously moderate, including, as they did, horses, hospitality, travel, Art, and at least the common decency of a jolly little motor of his own. He had often been warned by his uncle to spend the twenty thousand a year to which he was heir freely but not lavishly.

Why Sir Bryce Woodville had shown so sudden and marked an interest in a child he had known but for two months (and who had screamed most of that time), preferring him to a young man of talent and charm for whom he had shown indulgent affection for twenty-two years, was one of those mysteries that seem unsolvable in elderly gentlemen in general and in wicked uncles in particular. Sir Bryce had always been particularly fond of young people, and certainly greater youth and the nearer relationship were obviously the only points in which the son had the advantage over the nephew.

When Woodville found himself really hard up he sought a certain consolation in trying to do without things and in the strenuous hourly endeavour to avoid spending sixpence; no easy task to a man whose head was always in the clouds and his hand always in his pocket. As a novelty even economy may have its pleasures, but they are not, perhaps to all temperaments, either very sound or very lasting.

At the moment when omnibuses, cheap cigarettes, and self-denial were beginning to pall he had accepted the offer of the secretaryship, intending to look about to try to get something more congenial; perhaps to drift into diplomacy. Nothing could be less to his taste than the post of shorthandwriter to a long-winded old gentleman, to writing out speeches that in all probability would never be made, and copying pamphlets that would (most fortunately) never be printed. Often he thought he would rather "break stones on the road," drive a hansom cab, or even go on the stage, than be the superfluous secretary of such a dull, though dear nonentity.

Woodville also went in for painting: he had a little talent and a great deal of taste, sufficient, indeed, to despise his own work though he enjoyed doing it. In his leisure time he even tried to make money by copying old masters, and often sold them for quite amazing prices (amazingly low, I mean) to a few people who honestly preferred them to the originals on the undeniable grounds that they were at once cleaner and less costly. He was ambitious and knew he had brains and energy, besides being rather unusually well-turned-out in the matter of culture. And yet he had remained at Onslow Square for five years! As a career it was nothing. It could lead to nothing. Was there, then, some other attraction, something that outweighed, transcended for him all the petty pangs and penalties of his position?

This arch surmise of the writer will be found by the persevering reader to be perfectly reasonable and founded on fact.

CHAPTER III

A LOVE SCENE

There was a knock at the door. Woodville looked up. It was Sylvia.

Sylvia had that curious gift, abstract beauty, the sort of beauty that recalls vaguely some ideal or antique memory. Hence, at various times various people had remarked on her striking resemblance to Helen of Troy, Cleopatra, Dante's Beatrice, the Venus of the Luxembourg, one of Botticelli's angels, and La Giaconda!

Her head was purely Greek, her hair, fine in texture, and in colour golden-brown, grew very low in thick ripples on a broad forehead. The illusion of the remote or mythical was intensified by the symmetry of her slim figure, by her spiritual eyes, and beautiful, Pagan mouth. Tall and slender, her rounded arms and fine hands with their short pointed fingers seemed to terminate naturally in anything she held, such as a fan or flower, or fell in graceful curves in her lap. Sylvia had not the *chiffonnée* restless charm of the contemporary pretty woman; she did not, like Felicity, arouse with stimulating intensity one's sense of the modern.

Goddess, heroine, or angel she might be (her height, indeed, suggested heaven rather than hockey). Her beauty was of other days, not of the Summer Number. She was not, however, to do her justice, intentionally picturesque. She did not "*go in for the artistic style*"; that is to say, she did not part her hair and draw it over her ears, wear oddly-shaped blouses and bead necklaces, and look absent. The iron had obviously entered into her hair (or into every seventh wave, at least, of her hair), and her dresses fitted her as a flower its sheath. She was natural, but not in the least wild; no primrose by a river's brim, nor an artificial bloom, but rather a hothouse flower just plucked and very carefully wired. Hence she was at once the despair of the portrait painters, who had never as yet been able to help making her look on canvas like a bad Leighton in a Doucet dress, and the joy of the photographers, who in her honour set aside their pillars and their baskets of flowers, their curtains and their picture hats, being certain that she would pose herself exquisitely, and that her lines were so right that not even a photographer could improve on them.

Sylvia was so truly artistic in temperament and so extremely unpractical that it was not surprising she made an admirable housekeeper, having fortunately that inborn gift for organisation, and for seeing things on the whole, that is so much more important in home life than any small fussing about the unimportant details. And she would receive excuses from servants with a smile so sweet yet so incredulous that it disarmed deceit and made incompetence hide its head (or give notice).

She came round to the writing-table, bent her head over his shoulder, and said in a low voice of emotion, as though it were a secret—

"How are you getting on? Did you want me to find anything—an address, or anything?"

He put his hand on hers and looked up at her. Then he looked away.

"Don't, Sylvia. I wish you would go away. Or go to the other side of the room ... I can't stand it."

"Oh, Frank! How rude and unkind!" But she was apparently not offended, as she blushed and smiled while she moved a little away. Then she said, looking at the cards—

"Will the party be awful, do you think?"

"No, it won't be bad. Except for me, of course. To see you talking to other people. Not that I really care, because I know you have to. And besides, you won't, will you?"

"I promise I won't! I'll just be a hostess, and talk to old ladies, or stray girls, or perhaps just a few dull old married men."

"I approve of that programme. But—of course I have no right to advise, and I may be entirely wrong—supposing you were to leave out the old married men? You will have to talk to all the clever young men, I am afraid. Don't go to supper with F. G. Rivers. That's all I ask. I couldn't bear it."

"F. G. Rivers! Of course not! Felicity will do all that sort of thing. She has a talent for celebrities—like papa. But why on earth *mustn't* I go to supper with just F. G. Rivers?"

"Oh, I don't know. You can if you like. *I* don't care," said Woodville jealously.

"I thought he was a wonderfully clever novelist, tremendously successful and celebrated!"

"Yes, I know. That's what I meant," Woodville said.

"Aren't his books rather weird and uncanny ... and romantic,—all about local colour, and awfully cynical?"

"How well you know what to say about things! *Weird!* Delightful! I dare say that's what Rivers would expect a nice girl to say of his books. He spends half his time being afraid people should think his work is lurid, and the rest in being simply terrified that people should think it's not. He's very clever really, and a delightful companion."

"Is he cynical?" she asked.

"He's so sceptical, that he believes in everything, but especially hard work, like table-turning, crystal-gazing, and Sandow's exercises.... I was at Oxford with him, you know," Frank added explanatorily.

"I see, it's an old affection. Anybody else I'm not to speak to?"

"Nonsense, Sylvia; I want you to be charming to every one, of course. I believe in that sort of thing. It's the right atmosphere for a party. Don't think about *me*."

"How can I help it?"

Her grey eyes were reproachful.

Woodville looked into them, then abruptly looked away.

"What are you going to wear, Sylvia?"

"My white satin, I think. Do you like it? Or don't you?"

"No; it makes you look too much like a Gainsborough—or no, more like a Sargent—which is worse. I mean worse for me, of course."

"Oh, dear! why am I always *like* something? Well, what am I to wear, Frank? I've just ordered a sort of fluffy grey chiffon—like a cloud."

"Wear that. You're always in the clouds, and I'm always looking up at them.... I hope it has a silver lining?"

"Perhaps it has. I don't know yet, it hasn't come home. Felicity's going to wear a sort of Watteau-ish dress, pink and white and blue, you know. Of course, she won't wear any jewels—she never will. You see, Chetwode has such a lot of old ones in his family. She says she's afraid, if she did, the *Perfect Lady* or *Home Chirps* might say 'Lady Chetwode as usual appeared in the "Chetwode emeralds"'—or something idiotic of that sort."

"How like her! Then just wear your string of pearls."

"Mayn't I wear the little turquoise heart that you—didn't give me, the one I bought in the Brompton Road and gave it to myself from you, so that I could honestly say you hadn't?"

"Better not, Sylvia. It looks as if it came out of a cracker. And we don't need any symbols and things, do we?"

"Very well.... I'm afraid, Frank ... I shall have to go now."

Woodville looked hurt.

"What? Already! Then why did you waste the precious minutes alone in making epigrams about F. G. Rivers? He's such a good fellow too, I always got on with him at Oxford."

"Did I make epigrams? How funny! I didn't know I could."

She came a little nearer. Woodville said in a low voice, rather quickly—

"You looked really divine just now through the window, with the hyacinths in your hands—like the goddess of something or other—spring, I suppose.... When I look at you, I understand all the old poetry. *To Amaryllis* and Herrick—and—you know."

"Dear Frank!... Am I to find an address?"

"You can't, dearest. There is no address. Besides, they've moved. And I found it myself ever so long ago."

She laughed.

"Oh, Frank!"

Woodville put his hand out and took hers.

"Oh, don't go just yet!" he said imploringly.

"Why, you told me to go away just now—or to the other side of the room!"

"Ah, but that was ages ago! Why, you haven't *been* here two minutes! You can't be in such a hurry.... Anyhow, come here a second."

She obeyed, and leant over his shoulder.... Then he said abruptly—

"Yes, you had better go."

Blushing, she glided away at once, without another word.

Woodville remained at the desk, looking a little pale, and frowning. He had a theory that he was a very scrupulous man, with a high sense of honour. It was a worrying theory.

With a sigh he returned to the invitation cards.

CHAPTER IV

"AUNT WILLIAM"

Mrs. William Crofton, the widow of Sir James's brother, was, in her own way, quite a personage in London; at least, in the London that she knew. We have already seen her in the photograph in Savile's possession taken some forty years ago (by Mayall and Son, at Brighton). She was now an elderly lady, and still occupied the large ugly house in South Audley Street, where the children remembered their Uncle Mary. Felicity, Sylvia, and Savile had chosen to reverse the order in which they were told to speak of their uncle and aunt. Felicity had pointed out that not only was Aunt William more like an uncle, but that by this ingenious device they dodged a kind of history lesson. The great object always was to counteract carefully any information conveyed to them during the time of their education. All historians and teachers alike were regarded as natural enemies from Pinnock to Plato. On the same principle, Savile would never eat *Reading* biscuits, because he feared that some form of condensed study was being insidiously introduced into the system. Boys had to be on their guard against any treachery of that kind.

If there were a certain charm in the exterior of this old house—solid and aggressively respectable—its interior gave most visitors at first a nervous shock. Aunt William still firmly believed æstheticism to be fashionable, and a fad that should be discouraged. Through every varying whim of the mode she had stuck, with a praiseworthy persistence, to the wax flowers under glass, Indian chessmen, circular tables in the centre of the room, surrounded by large books, and the rep curtains (crimson, with green borders) of pre-artistic days. Often she held forth to wondering young people, for whom the 1880 fashions were but an echo of ancient history, on the sad sinfulness of sunflowers and the fearful folly of Japanese fans. Had the poor lady been but a decade or two more old-fashioned she would have been considered quaint and up-to-date. (A narrow escape, had she only known it!)

She was a small, pointed person, with a depressing effect of having (perhaps) been a beauty once, and she regarded Sylvia and Felicity with that mingled affection, pride, and annoyance compounded of a wish to serve them, a desire to boast of them, and a longing to bully them that is often characteristic of elderly relatives. The only special fault she found was that they were too young, especially Sylvia. Mrs. Crofton did not explain for what the girls were too young, but did her best to make Sylvia at least older by boring her to death about etiquette, religion, politics, cooking recipes, and kindred subjects. Aunt William was one of those rare women of theory rather than practice who prefer a menu to a dinner, and a recipe to either. Indeed, recipes were a hobby of hers, and one of her pleasures was to send to a young housekeeper some such manuscript as the following:—

"To Make Elderberry Wine Required—

Half a peck of ripe elderberries.
One and a half gallons of boiling water.

To Each Gallon of Juice

Three pounds of loaf sugar,
Four cloves,
Six allspice.

Stalk the berries, put them into a large vessel with the boiling water, cover it closely, and leave for twenty-four hours," and so on.

To one person she was quite devoted—her nephew Savile.

One morning Aunt William woke up at half-past seven, and complained to her maid that she had had insomnia for twenty minutes. Having glanced at the enlarged and coloured photograph of the late William that decorated every room, she ordered a luncheon of roast mutton and rice pudding, rhubarb tart and cream, almonds and raisins, and oranges, thinking that this menu would be at once suitable and attractive to a boy of sixteen. In a more indulgent moment she then sent out for a large packet of milk-chocolate, and prepared to receive Savile at lunch.

When Savile arrived in his father's motor, Mrs. Crofton, who had been looking out for him at the window, ran up to her room (she could run when alone) and allowed him to be shown into the drawing-room by himself. Aunt William resented automobiles as much as she disliked picture postcards, week-ends, musical comedies, and bridge.

Savile walked up and down the enormous room, lost in thought, and scarcely observing his surroundings. He smiled slightly as he contemplated the portrait of Uncle Mary, who was represented as leaning rather weakly for support against a pedestal that looked by no means secure, with a heavy curtain and a lowering sky in the background.

"Jove! what short frock-coats those chaps wore!" thought Savile. "What rotters they must have been!"

"And so Lord Chetwode is out of town again?" Aunt William said, as they sat over dessert.

"Gone to Newmarket."

"I see in the *Morning Post* that your sister Sylvia was at Lady Gaskaine's last night. I suppose she was the belle of the ball." She offered him some preserved ginger.

"No, she wasn't. There's no such thing as a belle of the ball now, Aunt William. She danced with Heath and Broughton, of course, and Caldrey, and those chaps. Broughton took her to supper."

Aunt William seemed gratified.

"Curious! I recollect Lord Broughton in kilts when he was a little toddling pet of seven! His father was considered one of the most fascinating men of his day, my dear. What a beautiful place Broughton Hall is!" She pressed another orange on him.

"Oh, Sylvia's all right," said Savile, impartially declining the fruit and producing an aluminium cigarette-case. Aunt William, pretending not to see it, passed him the matches as if in a fit of absence of mind. As a matter of fact, Savile was really more at home with Aunt William than with any one, even his sisters.

"And now, my dear boy, tell me about yourself."

Savile took out of his pocket the envelope containing her photograph.

"I say, I took this out of the album last time I came," he said apologetically.

Aunt William almost blushed. She was genuinely flattered.

"But what's that—that green book I see in your pocket? I suppose it's Euclid, or Greek, or something you're learning."

"No, it's not; it's poetry. A ripping poem I've just found out. I know you like that sort of rot, so I brought it for you."

Her face softened. Savile was the only person who knew her romantic side.

"A poem!" she said in a lowered voice. "Oh, what is it about?"

"Oh, about irises, and how 'In the Spring a Young Man's Fancy,' that sort of thing—Tennyson, you know."

"Tennyson!" exclaimed Aunt William. "Do you know Eliza Cook? I think 'The Old Armchair' one of the loveliest poems in the language."

"Never heard of it."

"Savile," said Aunt William, when they were sitting by the fire in the drawing-room, "I'm glad you're fond of poetry. Have you ever written any at all? You needn't be ashamed of it, my dear boy, if you have. I admire sentiment, but only up to a certain point, of course."

"Well, it's odd you should say that. I wrote something yesterday. I say, you won't go and give it away, Aunt William?"

"Most certainly not!"

She grew animated.

"Show it to me, if you have it with you. A taste for literature is in the family. Once a second cousin of ours—you never knew him—wrote me a sonnet!"

"Did he, though? Well, I dare say it was all right. Here's my stuff. I rather thought I'd consult you. I want to send it to some one."

Concealing his nervousness under a stern, even harsh demeanour, Savile took out a folded sheet of paper from a brown pigskin letter-case.

Aunt William clasped her hands and leaned forward.

Savile read aloud in an aggressive, matter-of-fact manner the following words:——

"My singing bird, my singing bird,Oh sing, oh sing, oh sing, oh sing to me,Nothing like it has ever been heard,"

(Here he dropped the letter-case, and picked it up, blushing at the contents that had fallen out.)

"And I do love to hear thee sing."

His aunt looked a little faint. She leant back and fanned herself, taking out her smelling-salts.

"That's not all," said Savile. Warming to his work, he went on more gruffly:—

"What should I do if you should stop?Oh wilt thou sing for me alone?For I will fly to hear your notes:Your tune would melt a heart of stone."

"My gracious, my dear, it's a poem!" said Aunt William.

"Who said it wasn't? But you can't judge till you've heard the whole thing."

She turned away her head and struggled with a smile, while he read the last verse defiantly and quickly, growing rather red:—

"I haven't got a stony heartOr whatever it is, it belongs to you:I vow myself thy slave,And always I shall e'er be true!"

There was an embarrassed pause.

"Well, I really think that last line is rather pretty," said Aunt William, who had regained her self-control. "But do you think it is quite—"

"Is it all right to send to Her?" he said. "That's the point!"

"Well, I can hardly say. Would your father———"

"I say! You're not going to tell the Governor?"

"No, never, Savile dear. It shall be our secret," said Aunt William, reassuringly.

"Of course, I know this sort of thing is great rot," he said apologetically, "but women like it."

"Oh, do they really?" said Aunt William. "Well! what I always say is, if you're born with a gift, you should cultivate it!"

Savile (thinking this encouragement rather meagre) replaced the poem and said: "I shall have to be going now, Aunt William. Got an appointment."

"With whom, my dear?"

"Yes," said Savile dryly. He did not approve of this direct method of ascertaining what one wants to know. He would confide, but never answered questions. She accepted the hint, but would not acknowledge it.

"Ah, I see!" she said knowingly (wishing she did). "Well, if you must go, you must!"

"Yes, Aunt William."

"But before you go, about that party ... I'm coming, of course. In fact, I'm having my peach brocade done up. Tell dear Sylvia that if there's anything I can do—I mean in the way of helping her with regard to the supper———"

"We've telephoned to Benoist's. It's all fixed up. Thanks very much."

"Oh! But still I think I'll send my recipe for salmon mayonnaise. Don't you think I might?"

"It can't do any harm, when you come to think of it," he answered, getting up.

Before he left, Aunt William pressed a sovereign into his hand guiltily, as if it were conscience money. He, on his side, took it as though it were a doctor's fee, and both ignored the transaction.

"Tell your father I'm sure I shall enjoy his entertainment, though why on *earth* he still lives in Onslow Square, when he ought to be in London, I can't and never shall, understand. However, I believe there's quite a sort of society in Kensington, and no doubt *some* of the right people will be there. Are any of the Primrose League coming, do you know, Savile?"

"Sure to be. There's Jasmyn Vere for one."

"Oh, Lord Dorking's son. He's a Knight Harbinger."

"Is he, though? He looks like a night porter," said Savile. "Good-bye." He then turned back to murmur. "I say, Aunt William. Thanks most awfully." She went back smiling.

A few minutes later Savile was looking over the railings into Berkeley Square.

In a kind of summer-house among the trees sat a little girl of fourteen dressed in grey. She wore a large straw hat on her head and a blue bow in her hair, and had evidently provided herself with materials of amusement for the afternoon, for she had a "picture-postcard album" by her side, and seemed absorbed in a thick volume of history.

Dolly Clive resembled in expression and the shape of her face one of Sir Joshua's angel's heads (if one could imagine them brunettes). She had large brown eyes and a long black plait, and was a graceful example of what was formerly called "the awkward age." It needed no connoisseur to see that she was going to be a very pretty woman. When she saw Savile, she rushed to the gate and let him in with a key.

"Hallo, Dolly!"

"I say, Savile, wasn't King Charles the Second an angel? I've just been reading all about him, and you can't think what fun they used to have!"

He seemed surprised at this greeting, walked slowly with her to the arbour, and said rather suspiciously——

"Who had fun?"

"Why Lady Castlemaine, and Nell Gwynne, and the Duchess of Portsmouth,—and all those people. It says so here, if you don't believe it! I wish I'd lived at that time."

"I don't. There's fun now, too."

"Ah, but you don't know anything about it, Savile. I bet you anything you like you can't tell me those clever lines about the poor darling King's death!"

"Of course I can. Everybody knows them." Savile made an effort and then said, "You mean Fain would I climb but that ..."

"Oh no, no, no! Oh, good gracious, no! One more try, now."

"Had I but served my God as faithfully as I have served my king ..."

"Wrong again. That's Sir Philip Sidney," she said, shutting up the book with a bang. "It's

Here lies our Sovereign Lord the KingWhose word no man relies on ..."

"I say, old girl, I didn't come here to talk history, if you don't mind."

"Well, what do you want to talk about? Shall I show you my new one of Zena Dare?" said Dolly, opening the postcard album.

"Certainly not. I can't worry about Zena Dare. No, I've got something to tell you—something rather serious. Zena Dare, indeed! What next?"

"Oh dear, are you in a bad temper?"

"How like a woman! No, I'm *not* in a bad temper. Talking sense doesn't show that one's in a bad temper. But it's a beastly thing to have to do."

Dorothy sat on both the books, came nearer to Savile, and looked rather pale, tactfully waiting, in silence.

Then suddenly he said in a different tone, quite cheerily——

"That's rather jolly, the way that blue bow is stuck in your hair, Dolly."

"I thought you wanted to talk sense, Savile. What is it? Have you found out—anything?"

"What do you mean? Yes, I've jolly well found out that I can't be engaged to you any more. I've no right to be."

She did not seem overwhelmed by the news.

"Fancy! Just fancy! Oh—I see. Is there some one else? Who is it, Savile?"

He smiled in his most superior way.

"My dear child, people don't go about mentioning women's names. Now look here, Dolly, I meant to be straight, so I told you right out."

She smiled.

"I wonder what sort of girl she is! Well, it can't be Gladys: she's much too hideous. That's *one* comfort!"

"You're right, it can't. Besides, it's not."

"Well, Savile, you're a dear good boy to come and tell me about it. And, the fact is, I was just wanting to tell you myself that perhaps we had better not be engaged any more. Just be pals instead, you know."

"Who's the man?" He spoke sternly.

She began to talk very volubly.

"You know those people whom we met at Dinard last summer, the de Saules? They're French, you know. Well, Madame de Saules,—you can't think how pretty she is,—and dear little Thérèse, and Robert have just come over here for the season. Thérèse is such a darling. You would love her. Only a kid, of course, you know, but...."

"And what price this beastly French boy? Now, listen to me. Foreigners are all rotters. I can tell you that if you're engaged to him you'll live to regret it. I speak as a friend, Dolly."

"Oh dear no! We're not engaged! You don't understand! Private engagements are not the proper thing in France. It isn't done. *Oh* no! Why, his mother would write to my mother and then he would send a bouquet, or something, and then———"

"A bouquet! By Jove! Why, you're more prehistoric than Aunt William! Well, look here, if this little blighter keeps his place I shan't interfere. But, mind you, if I see the smallest sign of———"

He rose to his feet.

"Of what?" said Dolly, rising and looking angry. "He's a nice, handsome, polite, dear boy. So there!"

"I should only wring his neck, that's all. Good-bye, old girl."

They walked to the gate together.

"It's only for your good, you know, Dolly. I don't mean to be a brute."

"Oh, it's all right, Savile."

"Dolly, dear."

"Yes, Savile."

"I'm awfully fond of you, really."

"Of course, I know, dear boy. Come again when you can, won't you?"

"*Won't* I?" said Savile.

CHAPTER V

ARTHUR MERVYN AT HOME

Sometimes Sir James would confide in his secretary, and become after dinner—he drank port—pompously communicative on the subject of the alliances his daughter might contract—if she would. As he became more and more confidential in fact, he would grow more and more distant in manner, so that if they began dinner like old friends, they seemed gradually to cool into acquaintances; and at the end of the evening—such an evening!—Woodville felt as if they had barely been introduced, or had met, accidentally, in a railway train. Yet he courted these *tête-à-tête* as one perversely courts a certain kind of suffering. At least, Sir James talked on the *only* interesting subject, and Woodville was anxious to know everything about his rivals; for, though he believed in Sylvia's affection, he was subject to acute, almost morbid, attacks of physical jealousy. To see other men admire her was torture, particularly as he had to efface himself and be treated by her father as a faithful vassal.

And he really disliked deceiving Sir James, whose open liking was evident and who thought him matrimonially as much out of the question as the gardener.

"Hang it all, Woodville's a gentleman!" Sir James would have cried furiously at any suggestion that it was imprudent to leave the young man and Sylvia so much together. Sir James always remembered that Woodville was a gentleman and forgot that he was a man.

Men who indulge in inexpensive cynicism say that women are complex and difficult to understand. This may be true of an ambitious and hard woman, but nothing can be more simple and direct than a woman in love.

Sylvia suffered none of Woodville's complications. She did not see why he should want to run away with her, still less why he should run away from her. Nothing could be wrong in her eyes connected with her love, for it was also her religion. Like most girls who can love at all, her life consisted, in fact, of this emotion only. She might go to the stores, wave her hair, buy new hats, ride in the Park, order dinner for her father (with great care, for he was a gourmet), read innumerable books (generally falling back on Swinburne and Ella Wheeler Wilcox), receive and meet innumerable people, go to the opera, and do many other agreeable, tedious, or trivial things; but her life was her love for Woodville. And she had all the courage and dignity of real self-surrender. Whatever he did was right. Whatever he said was clever. Everything was perfect, so long as he was *there*. To his scruples, despairs, delights, and doubts she always answered that, after all, they were only privately engaged, like heaps of people. And since Woodville had this peculiar—she secretly thought insane—objection to marrying her because she was an heiress and he was poor, then they must wait. Something would happen, and all was sure to come right. She did not wish to tell her father of the understanding at present, because she feared Woodville would probably have to go away at once. They would tell him when she was twenty-one. Only one year, and everything would be open and delightful.

A strong motive that kept Woodville there was jealousy. Sylvia, discreet as she was—no sparkling, teasing coquette—had yet all the irresistible magnetism of a woman who is obviously made for tenderness. But she showed as much deftness in keeping back her admirers as most girls do in attracting them. She had curious deep delicacies; she disliked nothing so much as to feel or show her power as a woman. Pride or vanity was equally out of the question in her love; it was unselfish and yet it was not exacting, as unselfish love generally is. So far as she knew, no unselfishness was required from him. With the unconscious cruelty of innocence she had kept him in this false position for years, looking happily forward to a rose-coloured future.

Was it consistent that, with all his scruples, Woodville had drifted into this romance?

A lovely girl of twenty and a remarkably good-looking young man of twenty-eight meeting every day, every moment, at every meal—she, romantic; he, the most impressionable of materialists! Surely nothing could be expected but (for once) the obvious!

The Greek banker, Mr. Ridokanaki, said to be one of the richest men in England, had of late begun to pay Sylvia what he considered marked attention. Huge baskets of flowers, sometimes in the form of silver ships, sometimes of wicker wheelbarrows, or of brocaded sedan-chairs, and filled with orchids, lilies, roses, everything that, in the opinion of a middle-aged banker, would be likely to dazzle and delight a nice young girl, were sent periodically to Onslow Square. These floral tributes flattered Sir James and Savile; Woodville said they were hideous; and Sylvia (who neither wrote to thank their sender nor even acknowledged them) always had them conveyed immediately to the housekeeper's room. The Greek's intention of marrying Sylvia was in the air. Woodville, Sylvia, and Savile were perhaps the only people who doubted the event's coming off. Ridokanaki was a small, thin, yet rather noticeable-looking man of fifty, with courteous cosmopolitan manners. He had a triangular face, the details of which were vague though the outline was clear, like a negative that had been left too long in the sun.

His slight foreign accent suggested diplomacy rather than the City; he was a man of the world, had travelled everywhere, and had the reputation of knowing absolutely everything. He was firm but kind—the velvet hand beneath the mailed fist—irritatingly tactful, outwardly conventional, *raffiné*, and rather tedious.

He called occasionally on Thursdays (Sylvia's day). Woodville was usually having jealous palpitations in the library while Ridokanaki talked strong, vague politics with Sir James, and drank weak tea poured out by Sylvia (who always forgot that he never took sugar). After these visits the powerful will of the Greek seemed to have asserted itself without a word. It was his habit to express all his ideas in the most hackneyed phrases except when talking business, so that he seemed surprisingly dull and harmless, considering how much he *must* know, how much he must have seen and done. He had practically made his immense fortune, and many people said that in his own line he was brilliant. It was also often said of him (with surprise), "all the same Ridokanaki is a very simple creature, *when you know him*." No one, however, had ever yet really known him quite well enough to prove or justify this description.

In the cumbrous continental fashion he was working up to the point of a proposal, and something seemed to herald his future success. The servants were all looking forward to the wedding. Only Price, the footman, sometimes put in a word for poor Mr. Woodville. To say that the romance was known and discussed with freedom in the servant's hall should be needless. The illusion that domestics are ever in the dark about what we fondly suppose to be our little secrets is still immensely prevalent among persons who are young enough to know better.

"All I can say is, that's the man I'd marry if *I* were a young lady, whether or no," Price would say, sometimes adding, "With all his flowers and motors, what *is* the other gent after all but a sort of foreigner? Mr. Woodville is the nephew of an English baronet. Give me an Englishman!"

To this the housemaid would reply—

"Foreigner or no foreigner, Miss Sylvia is no fool; and, mark my words, she would look all right in that house in Grosvenor Square!"

These dark sayings silenced Price, but they did not succeed in chilling his romantic enthusiasm, though the other servants took the more worldly view. Much as they liked Woodville, it could not be forgotten that Ridokanaki had the agreeable habit (at times practised by Jupiter with so much success) of appearing invariably in a shower of gold. Trillionaire though he was, no hard-up nobleman could be more lavish, especially in small things. Nowadays the romance of wealth is more fascinating than the romance of poverty, even in the servants' hall. And Ridokanaki was not, as they remarked, like one of those mere parvenus from South Africa or America. Belonging to an old Greek family of bankers who had been wealthy for generations, he had recently made a personal position that really counted in European politics. It had been rumoured that he might have married into a Royal if not particularly regal family. What he had done for Greece and England was hinted at, not generally known.

Sylvia's impersonal attitude, so obviously genuine, was a refreshing change to a man who had been for years invited with so much assiduity and who knew that he was still regarded in London not without hope as a splendid match. Surely, he would suddenly turn round, settle down, and look for a refined and beautiful wife to be head of his house.

There was a feeling in the air that Sir James's party, with its White Viennese Band, its celebrities, and general elaborate preparations, was really intended to be a background for the declaration. Undoubtedly, he would propose that night. All Sylvia thought about was, that she meant to wear the grey chiffon dress that Woodville liked, and he would think she looked pretty. She intended to conceal the little turquoise heart that she had bought herself (*from him*) in the Brompton Road in her dress, and to tell him about it afterwards.

To Felicity, the party was, like all entertainments, a kind of arena. What is commonly called flirting, and what *she* called bowling people over, she regarded as a species of field-sport. Her heart might ache a little under the Watteau-ish dress, because it appeared that nothing on earth would induce darling Chetwode to return from Newmarket. When Sylvia said gently she feared wild horses would not persuade him to come back, Felicity answered, with some show of reason, that wild horses were not likely to try. Indeed, little Felicity was rather depressed. What was the fun of bowling people over, like so many ninepins, unless dear Chetwode, her usual admiring audience, were there to see them overthrown? However, no doubt, it would be fun. Felicity's view of life was that it was great fun. As she had never had any real troubles, she had not yet discovered that a sense of humour adds acutely to one's sufferings at the time, though it may help recovery. To see the absurdity of a grief increases it. It entirely prevents that real enjoyment in magnifying one's misfortunes in order to excite sympathy—an attribute so often seen in women, from char-woman to duchess. But Felicity was not destined to misfortune. Ridokanaki sometimes compared her to a ray of sunshine, and her sister to a moonbeam. The comparison, if not startlingly original, was fairly just. Felicity retorted by saying that the Greek was like a wax-candle burnt at both ends and in the middle, while Woodville resembled a carefully shaded electric light. She was anxious to know the words in which

Ridokanaki would propose, and had already had several rehearsals of the scene with her sister, inducing Sylvia sometimes to refuse and sometimes to accept, just to see how it went. Felicity said that if he were rejected the marriage would in the end be a certainty, as a little difficulty would gratify and surprise him, and make him "*bother about it*" more. Everything was generally made so easy for him that he would certainly enjoy a little trouble, and the idea of obtaining a girl rather against her inclination would be sure to appeal to him. Opposition in such matters is always attractive to a spirited second-rate man.

All the preparations being complete, Woodville, part of whose absurd duties was to make quantities of unnecessary lists and go over the wine, went, the day before the party, to see a friend of his, where the atmosphere was so entirely different from his own that he regarded these visits as a change of air.

"Mr. Mervyn in?"

"Oh yes, sir. There's a rehearsal to-day. So Mr. Mervyn has lunched early."

A deep voice called from the inner room—

"Hallo, Frank! Come in, old chap!"

Arthur Mervyn had been at school and at Balliol with Woodville, and was one of his favourite companions. The only son of a great tragic actor, he possessed much of the genius of his late father, from whom he inherited, also, his finely-cut features, like some old ivory carving, his coal-black hair, and that sweet, humorous, yet sardonic smile that relieved, like a sparkle in dark waters, his somewhat sinister good looks.

Arthur Mervyn lived in a large, luxuriously furnished flat in Bloomsbury. The decorations were miracles of Morris: obviously they dated back about twenty years ago. Mervyn was not, however, a young man who was keen about his surroundings: he was indifferent to them; they had been chosen by his father, to whom background and all visible things had been of the first importance. The faintly outlined involuted plants on the wall-papers, the black oak friezes and old prints gave Arthur neither more nor less pleasure than he would have received from striped silk, white paint, and other whims of Waring. There were no swords, foils, signed photographs of royalties, pet dogs, or babies, invitation cards on the mantelpiece, nor any of the other luxuries usually seen in illustrated papers as characteristic of "Celebrities at Home". A palm, on its last legs, draped in shabby green silk, was dying by the window. The gloom was mitigated by an air of cosiness. There were books, first-rate and second-hand. Books (their outsides) were a hobby with Mervyn. Smoking in this den seemed as natural as breathing, and rather easier, though its owner never touched tobacco. On the Chesterfield sofa there was one jarring note. It was a new, perfectly clean satin cushion, of a brilliant salmon-pink, covered with embroidered muslin. Evidently it was that well-known womanly touch that has such a fatal effect in the rooms of a young man.

Woodville found Mervyn neither studying a part, reading his notices, nor looking in the glass. He had, as usual, the noble air of a student occupied with an Idea, and seemed absorbed.

"I say, Woodville, what do you think I've got?"

"A piece of rope that somebody wasn't hanged with?" asked Woodville. Arthur's curious craze for souvenirs of crime was a standing joke with them both.

"Better than that, old chap!" Mervyn spoke slowly, and always paused between each sentence. "What do you think I did yesterday? You know Jackson—chap who murdered people in a farm? I found out where he went to school in the north of England—and I said to myself—this fellow must have been photographed in a group as a boy."

There was a pause, disproportionately long.

"Sort of thing you *would* say to yourself," said Woodville a little irritably, as he lit a cigarette.

"Yes!—I took the 2.15—awful train. I went up there and went all over the school, called at the photographers—and actually got the group! And—there you are!"

Mervyn seemed very animated on the subject, and clapped his friend several times on the back with short, delighted laughs.

"By Jove!" said Woodville, looking at the photograph.

"Why do you say 'By Jove!'?" asked Mervyn suspiciously.

"Why? Well! I must say *something*! You always show me things on which no other comment is possible but an exclamation, or you tell me things so unanswerable that there's nothing to say at all."

"So I do," admitted Mervyn, smiling, as he locked away the souvenir. Then he sat down, and his animation dropped to a calmness bordering on apathy.

"And how are you getting on?"

"Not at all."

"Aren't you, though?" Mervyn pushed the matches sympathetically towards his friend, and seemed to fall into a reverie. Then he suddenly said, brightly: "I say, Woodville, you want cheering up. Come with me and see...."

"My dear chap, I'm not in the mood for theatres."

"Frank!" His friend looked at him with hurt reproach. "As though I'd *let* you see me in this new thing they're bringing out! No.—But I've got a seat at the Old Bailey for to-morrow morning to see the trial;—I think I could take you."

Woodville smiled.

"I appreciate immensely your methods of cheering people, Arthur, and I know what that offer is from you. But I really don't care about it."

"Don't you?—What *do* you care about?"

Woodville was silent. Then Mervyn said suddenly, "I say, how's Miss Crofton and her sister? I like little Lady Chetwode awfully. She's a pretty little thing, awfully amusing, and quite clever.—She's very keen on crime, too, you know."

"Oh no, nonsense, Arthur! She only pretends to be, to humour you. It's chaff. She hates it, really."

"Hates it! Does she, though?—Well, anyhow she promised to go with me to the Chamber of Horrors one day. Make up a party, you know. And she says she thinks all the criminals there have the most wonderful faces physiognomically; benevolent foreheads, kindly eyes, and that sort of thing; and then she said, well, perhaps any one *would* look good with such lovely complexions as they have! She says *she* would have been taken in! She would have engaged all the Hannahs—she says that murderesses are always called Hannah—as housekeepers, they looked so respectable—except for the glassy eye. Oh, we had a long talk. Yes, and she'll bring her sister. You might come, too, one afternoon."

"Oh, of course I'll come. It would be rather jolly," said Woodville.

"Well, when this new thing is once out we'll fix it up, eh? I shall see Lady Chetwode to-morrow—at your party."

"Oh, are you coming?"

"Oh, yes I'm going. Every one's going."

At this moment they heard outside the house a tremendous uproar, the snorting, panting, puffing, and agonised throbbing that could only proceed from a motor in distress.

"Who's that?" said Woodville, going to look out of the window.

Mervyn closed his eyes and leant back in his chair.

"It's nothing," he said. "It's Bertie—Bertie Wilton, you know."

"Oh! Good. Bertie's always exhilarating."

CHAPTER VI

AN AGREEABLE RATTLE

A moment later there entered the room a slim, good-looking young man of about twenty-five years old, whose eyes were very bright and whose clothes were very smart, and who gave the impression of being at once in the highest spirits and at least a year in advance of the very latest expression of the mode. He was very fair, clean shaven, with smooth blond hair, white teeth, and the most mischievous smile in London.

Bertie Wilton had the reputation of being the wittiest of all the dandies, but his one great weakness was a mania for being *dans le mouvement*, and a certain contempt for any ideas, however valuable, that had been suggested earlier than, say, yesterday afternoon. Extremely good-natured, lively, and voluble, he was immensely popular, being considered, as indeed he was, one of the last of the conversationalists. He might be frivolous, but he was always interesting. He could talk about anything—and he did.

"I didn't know you'd got a motor, Bertie," said Woodville.

Wilton looked at it lovingly out of the window, arranged the gardenia in his button-hole, and said—

"Oh yes! I'm mad on motors. I've had three! This is my new toy. It's a ripper, the only *right* kind. It *can* go, I'll say that for it. I've been fined twice for exceeding the speed limit already."

"But you've never done anything else," said Woodville.

Bertie laughed.

"Ah! no; perhaps not. Well, anyway, I simply love it. I haven't even come here this morning *merely* to see you, Mervyn, or on the off-chance of meeting old Woodville, but simply to try the new Daimler before lunching in it—at least, not exactly lunching *in* it, but *with* it,—no, no, not *with* it, you know what I mean—with the dearest old gentleman who lives in the wilds of West Kensington. He's simply devoted to me. Why, I can't think. But he's got a sort of idea that I saved his life on a hill near Hastings. What really happened was, that his idiot of a chauffeur had utterly smashed up the car, and he and the old gentleman were sitting on the Downs with every probability of remaining there for the rest of their natural lives!"

"And this, I suppose, is where you came in," said Woodville.

"Rather! I was spinning along from Brighton, and I saw those poor creatures in their pitiable position. To hop out of the motor, have an explanation with the old gentleman (who was stone deaf, by the way), to persuade him to come with me, to drive him to his *intensely* comfortable and charming country house in the heart of Hastings, and to send for a surgeon to attend to the internal injuries of the car, was, for me, the work of a moment! I made up quite a romance about the old gentleman. You're a reading man, Woodville, and so you know, from books, that the slightest politeness to an eccentric millionaire sets you up in gilded luxury for life, don't you? I expected, of course, that he would cut off his family with a shilling, and would leave me at the *very* least £20,000 a year. Isn't it funny, my being wrong? It turned out that he neither could nor would do anything of the sort. He was neither eccentric nor a millionaire—though he was very well off and very clever. But, perhaps you ask yourself, had he a lovely daughter, whose hand he would offer me in marriage? Not he! He has only a hideous married son and daughter-in-law who live in Manchester, and all I've got out of the adventure, so far, is lunching with him, and talking to him, and heaps of practice in shouting; he's so deaf. Besides, he's a dear."

"What a wonderful chap you are! The last time I saw you, weren't you secretary to a foreign Duke, with a brilliant diplomatic future before you, or something?" said Woodville, while Mervyn appeared to be lost in thought.

"I know, but that was *last* season! Lots of people are just as keen as I am, you know. Broughton, for instance, has actually invented a car of his own. I once permitted myself to speak rather disrespectfully of Broughton's quite ridiculous car, and, of course, some kind friend told him practically every word I said; and he was quite hurt. We had a regular sort of scene about it."

"What did you say against the car?" said Mervyn judicially, waking up.

"Well, I may be wrong, but it seems to me that it isn't an ideally convenient arrangement (particularly for ladies) to have to climb into a motor, by means of a ladder, over the back! I understood that though Broughton's design had all sorts of capital new arrangements with regard to cushions and clocks and looking-glasses, and mud-guards, he had, *most* unfortunately, quite forgotten the door.

"Well, we met at the Bellairs' Fancy Ball (I went as Louis the Nineteenth) last week, you know, and had an explanation, and sort of made it up, but I'm afraid, like that uncomfortable old king, though he smiled at the jest, he never forgave the satire.

"I say, I must fly now. I have to lunch with the old gentleman. Can I drop you anywhere, Woodville?"

"I've got to be at the theatre at one, to rehearse," said Mervyn suddenly.

"Then you must be quick, old boy. It's a quarter to two now," said Bertie.

They took their leave.

After many tender inquiries after its health from the chauffeur, Bertie sprang into the motor with Woodville, and they started off.

"I say, Woodville," began Bertie, as they spun along, "I want to talk about Lady Chetwode. I'm awfully in love with her."

"Didn't know you knew her."

"I don't. That's nothing to do with it. You can be awfully in love with a person you don't know. In fact, I believe *I* can be far more seriously devoted to a perfect stranger than to a woman I know personally. But I've often seen her at the Opera. And I'm *going* to know her. I'm going to be brought to your party to-morrow night by Mrs. Ogilvie. Didn't you know? Tell me, why isn't Chetwode ever *there?*"

"Don't be an ass! They're devoted to each other. Turtle-doves aren't in it."

Bertie's eyes sparkled.

"I *know*! I suppose he stays away for fear of her getting tired of him. Quaint idea. Never been done before quite like that. Well, it may be very clever, but I shouldn't do it! Frankly, I should always be there or thereabouts, at all risks! You don't seem to understand (knowing them so intimately, of course you wouldn't) what Lady Chetwode is going to be. Why, she's simply *the* person already. I hear of her everywhere, and the sister, Miss Crofton; I saw her too the other night. She's quite beautiful. I don't believe they know what to do with her."

"What on earth do you mean?" said Woodville.

"My dear boy, I have my faults, but I have one little gift, and that is a *flair* for success. It will be all very well for Miss Sylvia to marry the Greek man to begin with——"

"Do you propose she should marry any one else to go on with then?"

"Don't be absurd. I mean, of course, that would start her, and so on. He's a friend of exalted personages and that sort of thing, and it would certainly bring her forward. Although I think she could do better. But she ought to come out in tableaux or something and be really seen, quite soon; while she's a novelty."

"I really think there's something wrong with your tonneau," said Woodville.

Bertie smiled cheerfully. "Don't worry, my chauffeur's one of the best drivers in London. But, about tableaux; next month at Worcester House——"

"Miss Crofton doesn't care about that sort of thing," said Woodville.

"No? I heard she had rather a line of her own. What is her pose? She ought to settle on it. You know there is nothing so uncomfortable as not having settled on one's pose. Oh!" Bertie gave a start. "I beg your pardon. I see the whole thing! But of course! You're in love with her. What a fool I am!"

"You are indeed. I see very little of Miss Crofton. You're generally positive, and always wrong."

"Oh, is it as bad as that? My dear Woodville, I'm so sorry! What a tactless idiot I am! But Lady Chetwode, now. Her great friend, Vera Ogilvie, I know very well indeed. I met her last Tuesday, so she's quite an old friend. Mrs. Ogilvie's the pretty woman who thinks she has a Byzantine profile. She's all over strange jewels and scarabs, and uncut turquoises and things. She has a box on the second tier, and it was there that it all happened."

"That what happened?"

"Why, my falling in love at first sight; I mean, with Lady Chetwode, of course; and what makes me so bad is that I hear of her everywhere. Nothing worse than that! Her frocks and her mots,—it seems she's very clever, I hear, and says the most delightful things. And there's another thing, if I don't make a dash for it this season, I shan't have a chance next. I see that."

"Didn't I tell you she's simply wrapped up in her husband?"

"Of course. That's just the point. I don't know Chetwode, but he's the fellow who has the wonderful collection. First Empire things, and china, and all that. Besides, he goes racing. They say his horse has a chance of winning the Derby. Oh, you don't know what a distinguished family they are! Well, anyhow, you see he's busy, and if they *do* have honeymoons every now and then—as no doubt they do—I really hardly see what that matters to me."

"Frankly, nor do I," said Woodville.

"No, indeed; I like it better, because I don't mind telling you I've got heaps of things on just now."

"You look as if you had," said Woodville dryly.

"Is this meant for an attack on my tie? You'll be wearing one like it yourself in a fortnight! Mrs. Ogilvie's great fun. Yesterday she took me with her and a sort of country girl, a clergyman's daughter from Earl's Court, to buy a hat at Lewis's; (for the girl I mean). It was *extraordinary*! The girl isn't at all bad-looking, but naturally wears her hair *perfectly* flat, with a kind of knob at the back, the wrong kind. On the top of this the milliners stuck, first, the most enormous hat, eccentric beyond the dreams of the Rue de la Paix, all feathers, and said, Oh, quel joli mouvement, Madame! The poor girl, frightened to death, thinking the birds were alive, tore it off. So then they tried on those absurd, tiny, high, little things that require at least twenty-five imitation curls to keep them up, and show them off, and in which poor Miss Winter looked like an escaped lunatic. We tried everything in the shop, and at last Mrs. Ogilvie said, 'Perhaps we had better come again, later in the season, when the hats would be smaller, or not so large.'—Do you know Miss Winter? She has *rather* pretty red hair, and a dazed intellectual expression. She's the sort of girl who can only wear a sailor hat (I never saw a sailor in a straw), as they call them, or perhaps something considered picturesque in the suburbs; you know, with skyblue *crêpe de chine* strings under the chin. If she'd only been an athletic girl we could have gone straight to Scott's, and then we should have known where we were—but she's artistic, poor thing." Bertie smiled mischievously.

"Your valuable advice doesn't seem to have been much use, then?"

"*Rather* not! Especially as Mrs. Ogilvie has this craze about thinking she's Oriental (I wonder who put it into her head), and *would* order absurd beaded things, like Roman helmets, when of course she'd look delightful in a dark claret-coloured velvet sort of Gainsborough, with dull brown feathers. But women are so perverse. Look how they won't wear black when nothing suits them so well!"

"Won't they? I wonder you don't go into the millinery business. I think you'd do very well."

"Don't talk rot. I'm only interested as an amateur; it's art for art's sake. But I *do* understand frocks. I will say that I think women's dress is the only thing worth being really extravagant on. Don't you?"

"No, I don't."

They were now proceeding down Bond Street at a pace that the crowd compelled to be rather leisurely.

"There's Aunt William in her old-fashioned barouche with the grey horses. It's *such* a comfort to me, always, to see Mrs. Crofton; it makes one feel at least there is something stationary in this changeable world. Who's that boy looking at?—at you? Isn't it the Crofton boy?"

"Yes. Let's stop a minute; I want to speak to him."

Savile, seeing them, crossed the road, and said, before Bertie could begin—

"Extraordinary weather for the time of—year!"

"Come off the roof!" said Woodville, smiling. "What are you doing in Bond Street?"

"Oh, only going to Chappell's, the music shop, to get a song. One of those Sylvia doesn't sing," said Savile, looking straight at him.

"Oh, I know what it is," said Bertie; "it's Pale Hands that Burn, or Tosti's Good-bye!"

"No, it just isn't."

"Then it's something out of The Telephone Girl or something. Do tell us what it is. I hate these musical mysteries."

"It's not a mystery at all. It's Home sweet Home," said Savile.

They tried to persuade him to join them, but he walked off.

"Delightful boy," said Bertie, after a moment. "So correct. I'm sure he's *the* person at home, and spoilt, and does what he likes with them all, doesn't he? Of course, he's the person to be friends with if you want anything fixed up! Well, here we are at Onslow Square. It was jolly seeing you again. You must come for another longer spin soon. Isn't Mervyn a good chap? He's so really distinguished that it wouldn't ever matter what he wore, or where he went, or when. And you'd never *dream* he was an actor, would you?"

"Not unless you saw him act," said Woodville, getting out.

CHAPTER VII

THE NIGHT OF THE PARTY

Sir James was in one of those heroic moods that were peculiarly alarming to his valet. He was so abnormally good-tempered, and seemed so exceedingly elated about something, that it was probable he might suddenly, in Price's pathetic phrase, turn off nasty, or fly out.

As a matter of fact, Sir James was dominated by what are called mixed feelings. The letter that he read and re-read as he walked about his library enchanted him. But the appearance of that library was maddening. It had been transformed into a ladies' cloak-room. On his own writing-desk were an oval silver mirror, a large powder-puff, and several packets of hairpins. All trace of politics seemed to have been completely wiped out. Sir James thoroughly enjoyed picturing to himself Mr. Ridokanaki in this room on the following morning, asking for a blessing, on his knees, and to fancy himself saying solemnly, "Take her, my boy, she is yours!" or words to that effect.

Not only had the trillionaire sent Sylvia six feet of flowers in a gun-metal motor-car studded with sapphires, but Sir James, also, had received a respectful request (practically a species of royal command) for consent to his addresses. Ridokanaki stated that he had not as yet, of course, said anything to Sylvia, but proposed, unless her father objected, to try to win her fair hand that very evening. It was a triumph, even for Sylvia. Sir James laughed, as he only laughed when alone. But on looking up from the letter what he saw jarred on him. How he could well imagine the wrap that would be placed carelessly over the bust of Pitt in the corner, and all the cloaks and frivolous chiffons which would lie on that solemn study table! Rage had the upper hand. Sir James broke out, and rang the bell violently.

"Price, where's Miss Crofton? Tell her I want her immediately. This instant! Lose no time. But tell her on no account to hurry. In fact, any time will do as long as she comes at once. Wait a moment, wait a moment. Don't be so precipitate, Price. You leave the room before you hear your orders. I've had to speak to you about this before.... Is Miss Crofton dressed yet?"

"Yes, Sir James. Miss Crofton is quite ready. Lady Chetwode is with her."

"Oh! then tell her it doesn't matter. She needn't trouble."

"Yes, Sir James."

The sisters were standing in Sylvia's pale blue bedroom in front of the long mirror. Felicity's fair, almost silvery hair, puffed out round her wilful little face, looked as though it were *poudré*. She wore a striped brocade gown all over rosebuds, and resembled a Dresden china figure. Sylvia's exquisitely modelled face and white shoulders emerged from clouds of grey tulle.

"It's rather a shame, Sylvia; you'll bowl over everybody. Roy Beaumont will say you look mythological. Oh, and poor Mr. Ridokanaki! You'll refuse him to-night, I suppose! What fun it must be to be a pretty girl going about refusing people in conservatories—like a short story in a magazine! I've forgotten how I did it. In a year, darling? Quite. I say, have I overdone the dix-huitième business? Do I look like a fancy ball? Pass me a hairpin, dear. No, don't. I suppose you know that Chetwode has never seen this dress! What do you think of *that*? One would think we were an old married couple."

"Hardly, dear. Put it on to go and meet him at the station," said Sylvia, rather unpractically. "No, you're not too last-century. I think you look more like the next."

"Well, I hope so," said Felicity, fluttering a tiny Pompadour fan; "and if De Valdez says I look like a Marquise of the olden times, as he once did, I simply won't stand it. Let's go down. But first tell me what you will say when Mr. Rid ... Oh, bother, I can't say all that. Let us call him the man. 'Miss Crofton, might I respectfully venture to presume to propose to hope to ask to have a word with you? You are like a grey rose', or something or other."

"Oh, don't be absurd. Sometimes I think the whole thing is all your fancy, and Savile's."

"My fancy! Then what was that enormous, immense thing in the hall I fell over—a sort of tin jewelled bath, crammed with orchids and carnations? Frank Woodville was helping Price to cart it away, and trying to break some of the flowers by accident."

"Oh, was Mr. Woodville taking it away?" Sylvia smiled.

At that moment a firm knock at the door, and the words, "I say, Sylvia," announced Savile's entrance. He walked in slowly, brushed his sisters aside like flies, and stood looking at himself in the long mirror, which reached nearly from the ceiling to the floor. It was a solemn moment. He was wearing his very first evening-dress suit.

They watched him breathlessly. He carefully kept every trace of expression out of his face. Then he sat down, and said seriously to himself—

"Right as rain. You're all right, girls, too. Rather rot Chetwode not being here. Rather a pose, Felicity not wearing jewels. Why is the Governor in such a state? He's frightfully pleased about something. He flew out at me and said I ought to work for my button-holes, as he did. Really rather rot! I said, 'Well, father, a pink carnation's all right. The King wore one at Newmarket.' He said the *King* could afford it. Cheek! Sylvia, I say, you *are* all right! I'm going down."

Suddenly remembering his broken heart, Savile paused at the door, caught Felicity's eye, and sighed with an effort, heavily. Then, with his usual air of polite self-restraint, out of proportion to the occasion, he left the room.

Soon the White Viennese Band was tuning up, and the house, which was built like a large bungalow, decorated all over with crimson rambler rosebuds, looked very gay and charming. Sir James beamed as various names, more or less well known in various worlds, were incorrectly announced. Felicity went into a small room that had been arranged for conversation to see through the window that the garden had been artistically darkened for the occasion.

In the room were several men. Roy Beaumont the young inventor with his calm face and inscrutable air was looking up as he spoke to De Valdez, the famous composer. Roy Beaumont wore minute boot-buttons on his cuffs and shirt front.

De Valdez (more difficult to secure at a party than a Prime Minister) was a very handsome, unaffected, genial man who, though an Englishman, had much of the Spanish grandee in his manner and bearing. He had a great contempt for the smaller amenities of dress, and his thick curling hair made more noticeable his likeness to the portraits of Byron.

Felicity at once said, as if in great anxiety—

"You *mustn't* call me a Marquise of the olden time! Will you?" She smiled at the composer as Roy Beaumont went upstairs, leaving Felicity to begin the evening by trying the room with De Valdez.

Comparatively early, and quite suddenly, the rooms were crowded on the usual principle that no one will arrive till every one is there. They were filled with that inaudible yet loud chatter and the uncomfortable throng which is the one certain sign that a party is a success. The incorrect labelling of celebrities seemed to be an even more entrancing occupation than flirting to the strains of the Viennese Band. A young girl with red hair and eager eye-glasses, who had never in her life left Kensington, except to go to Earl's Court, entreated a dark animated young man who had just been introduced to her, but whose name she did not catch, to "sit down quietly and tell her all about everybody."

He amiably complied.

"That," he said, "that man with the white beard is Henry Arthur James. He writes all those books that no one can understand—and those clever plays, you know, that every one goes to see."

"Does he really? Fancy! Can you point me out the man who wrote, 'Oh the Little Crimson Pansies' and 'The Garden of Alice'? I love his work. It's so weird. F. J. Rivers, you know."

"My dear Miss Winter, what a dreadful thing! I'm afraid you'll be very disappointed. As a matter of fact, I am F. J. Rivers myself. Isn't it a pity? I'm so sorry. And I'm afraid I am not weird. Do forgive me. I'd be weird in a minute if I could. You know that, I'm sure. Don't you?"

"Fancy! Just fancy!" She blushed crimson. "I was being so natural. I had no idea I was talking to a clever person."

"No wonder!"

"You see, I'm interested in things. I particularly love the intellectual atmosphere of this house, and I read all the serious magazines and things, the *Bookman* and the *Saturday Review* and the *Sketch*; and so on."

"Should you say the atmosphere was really so intellectual here?" said Rivers a little doubtfully.

The Viennese Band was playing *Caresses* in its most Viennese way; people were gaily coming up from supper or coquettishly going down, or sitting in corners *à deux*, dreamily. The heavy scent of red rosebuds hung over all. So becoming was the background at this particular moment that nearly every woman looked fair and every man brave....

"I'm afraid—I mean, I suppose—you take what they call an intelligent interest in the subjects of the day, Miss Winter?"

"I should think so, indeed!" she answered.

"Oh dear!" Rivers looked depressed as he tried to remember what he knew about Radium and Russia.

"Somehow I don't feel frightened of *you*," she said. "Will you take me to have a cup of tea?"

He escorted her downstairs, endeavouring to make up for any disappointment she might feel by pointing out with reckless lavishness Mr. Chamberlain, Beerbohm Tree, Arthur Balfour, Madame Melba, Filsen Young, George Alexander, and Winston Churchill, none of whom, by a curious coincidence, happened to be present.

"Surely I may talk to you a moment," Woodville murmured to Sylvia. "Every one's happy eating, and you needn't bother. Just come out, one second—on the verandah through the little room. After all, I'm a friend of the family!"

"Why, so you are!"

She fluttered out with him through the French window of the little conversation room to a part of the garden that had been boarded and enclosed, forming with its striped awning and Japanese lanterns a kind of verandah. No one was in sight.

"This is the first second to-night I haven't been utterly wretched," said Woodville firmly.

"Oh, Frank! How kind of you to talk like that!"

"How beautiful of you to look like that!—And this is the sort of thing I have to stand—utterly ignored—I suppose you know I worship you? Do you really belong to me, Sylvia?"

"Oh, Frank! Why, I *love* you!"

"Do you really?"

"Of course. Look here, don't tell any one—not even yourself—but I'm wearing the little locket after all."

The kiss was short but disturbing. As they came down to earth with a shock, they saw, looking at them steadily through the half-open window, Mr. Ridokanaki. He seemed interested.

At a look from Sylvia Mr. Woodville faded away, feeling as if he were sneaking off. Sylvia went indoors.

"Good evening, Miss Crofton," said the harsh yet sympathetic pleasant voice; "I have been seeking you since this half-hour.... I was coming to ask if I might have the great honour of taking you to supper. Of course, it is an immense privilege—far more than I might expect. Still, may I venture to hope?"

"With pleasure," said Sylvia. She took his arm.

"It is very kind of you, Miss Crofton. What a very interesting face that young man has!"

"Which young man?" Sylvia asked innocently.

"The young man who was in the garden. I am sure he is clever. Your father's—er—secretary, I think? *What* did you say his name was, again?"

"His name is Mr. Woodville. Yes, I think he is clever. Quite an old friend, you know," Sylvia added rather lamely.

One could see no difference in the Greek, since he talked on in his usual urbane way, and made no allusion of any sort the whole evening, either to the floral tribute he had sent, to his letter to Sir James, or to the little scene he had interrupted.

In the supper-room all was gaiety and laughter.

"How hollow all this sort of thing is, isn't it?" said De Valdez, presenting Felicity with a plover's egg, as he passed carrying a plate laden with them to some one else.

"They do seem rather hungry, don't they? But why aren't you eating any supper, Mr. Wilton?"

Having done her duty to all her old friends, Felicity was occupying herself very congenially by steadily bowling over a completely new young man. It was Bertie Wilton, whom Mrs. Ogilvie had brought on the grounds that he could have danced if it had been a dance, and that he was the son of Lady Nora Wilton. Felicity was very much pleased with his condition. It seemed most promising, considering she had known him about a quarter of an hour.

"Supper! I should think two hot plates, one strawberry, and a sip of champagne more than enough for a person who is falling every moment more and more—Don't take that plover's egg, Lady Chetwode! It isn't fair! You have given me the sole right to provide for you this evening, and that man has no business to come interfering. Let him attend to his own affairs."

"He only dropped one plover's egg on my plate, as an old friend—out of kindness! He meant no harm," pleaded Felicity.

"Yes, that's all very well, but it was a liberty. It implies that I cannot provide you with all that you require. He must learn better." Mr. Wilton firmly removed the plover's egg and placed it on the next table, at which Rivers and the red-haired girl were still chattering volubly. Rivers immediately brought it back as lost property, courteously presenting it to Felicity on a silver salver.

"This is becoming unbearable! I shall have to write to the *Times*." Wilton gave the egg to a waiter and a furious glance at Rivers, and then sat down again. He was remarkably good-looking with his sparkling blue eyes and mischievous expression, and Felicity glanced at him with approval. He would do very well—for the evening. He was quite worth powder—and shot. At least, he was, to her, a perfect stranger, and there was a great dearth of spring novelties at the party to-night.

"I've been waiting for you for years," said Bertie Wilton in a soft, low, impressive voice.

"Fancy! How patient of you!—How did you know it was me?"

"Oh, instantaneous-sympathy, I suppose."

"On your side, do you mean? I should call it telepathy, or perhaps—conceit."

"Call it what you like. But how is it you're so wonderful? Tell me that."

"I can't think," she said dreamily.

"I'm certain I met you in a previous existence," continued the young man.

"What a good memory you must have, Mr. Wilton! It's as much as I can do to remember the people I meet in *this* existence. I believe I saw you in Mrs. Ogilvie's box at *Madame Butterfly*."

"I know, I saw you from there. I was rooted to the spot—I believe that's the right expression, though it sounds rather agricultural—while at the same time you might have knocked me down with a feather! It's really true, you might. But I know you wouldn't have, you're far too good and kind."

"I don't think I *had* any feathers with me," said Felicity.

Bertie went on. "But this life is so short.—Do you think it's worth it?—(Do have some mayonnaise.)—I mean the kind of thing one does—waiting, waiting—at last asking, for instance, to call on your day—only meeting in throngs—perhaps not getting a chance, for months, to tell——"

"I suppose life *is* rather long, isn't it?" Felicity said, as a concession.

"Then I may come and see you the day after to-morrow?" he asked.

"Not till the day after to-morrow!" she exclaimed in surprise. "Why wait so long?"

"At what time?" he persisted, smiling.

"You may call next Monday—at five. Not this week."

"That's impossible. I can't. It's too dreadful. I can't wait till Monday, I can't.... Well, let me come on Tuesday, then?"

"*I* see. You're particularly engaged on Monday. After all, why trouble? There are so many people for you to call on!"

"If I might call to-morrow, ONCE, I'll never be engaged again! I'll never call on any one else during the whole of my natural life."

"All right," she said absently. "Call to-morrow, ONCE, as you say. Not that I ever heard of any one calling twice the same day, at least not the first day."

"Oh, Lady Chetwode, how kind of you! Did you say five? Can't you make it half-past four?"

"Very well."

"Won't you make it three? I beg your pardon. I'll walk up and down in front of the house strewing flowers from three till half-past four and then come in, may I? And will there be crowds of people there?"

"Well, you haven't given me much time," said Felicity. "I'll try to get up a party by to-morrow, if you wish it."

"How can you be so unkind! Do you think me very pushing—and vulgar?"

"Very. No, only vulgar."

"At any rate, I'm sincere. It's like Tristan and Ysolde; at least, it's like Tristan. You can't look me straight in the eyes and tell me I'm not sincere!"

Felicity looked; and was quite satisfied.... How hard it was that Chetwode was not there for her to tell him all about the conversation going home! This thought vexed her so much that she became absent and lost spirit to keep it up.

Mr. Rivers had promised to send the red-haired girl, who had fallen hopelessly in love with him, his latest book. He had arranged to take her and her mother to a concert at the Queen's Hall the following Sunday afternoon.

Roy Beaumont was the centre of a crowd of interested people, chiefly bearded men, who paid him sportive homage, and pretty women, as he illustrated, by means of a wineglass, two knives, and a saltspoon, his new invention for having one's boots fastened by electricity, which was to do for Marconigrams, expose radium as a foolish fraud, and consign clock-work to limbo. "You don't touch the buttons and the invention does the rest," he pointed out.

Aunt William in her peach gown was taken down to supper by Jasmyn. He was a plump middle-aged young man, a very social person, and quite an arbiter on matters of fashion; known for his kindness and politeness to dear old ladies and shy young men. A romantic affection for a certain widow, whom his friends said he spoke of as "Agatha, Mrs. Wilkinson," to give the effect of a non-existent title, had prevented him, so far, from marrying. He was bland and plaintive, looked distinguished, supremely good-natured, and rather absurd.

"It is too marvellous," said Aunt William, as she ate her *foie-gras*. "What a collection my dear brother-in-law has assembled to-night. Half the people here I have never heard of in the whole course of my life!"

"And the other half," said Jasmyn, "you have perhaps heard of rather too often. No strawberries, Mrs. Crofton?"

"No thank you. I don't care for fruit, except in its proper season. My dear husband always said strawberries were not eatable till the fourth of June."

"Ah, how right he was!" said Jasmyn absently, eating a very large one. "I suppose he didn't care for *primeurs*. Personally, I admit that I am absolutely sick of asparagus by April, but I think it best to eat and drink as much as possible because I suffer so terribly from depression."

"Depression! Yes, you would. Having everything on earth you want, and being thoroughly spoilt, like all men of the present day, you would naturally have low spirits."

"Ah, I dare say you don't believe me. But I assure you, Mrs. Crofton, that under all my outward misery I generally have an aching heart.... How lovely Lady Chetwode's looking!"

"Lady Chetwode," said Aunt William loyally, "is a most brilliant woman. Her sister is a beautiful girl, and her brother Savile is doing well at Eton. His last report——"

"Do you know, I'm terribly frightened of Savile," said Jasmyn. "He's such a man of the world that I feel positively crude beside him."

Before the end of the evening, Ridokanaki took an opportunity to ask if Woodville would dine with him.

"I want to have a little talk with you," he said. "I have an idea—it may be perfectly wrong—that what I have to say may interest you."

Woodville accepted; surprised at his rival's cordiality.

"At Willis's, then, at eight, Mr. Woodville?"

"At eight. Thanks very much."

CHAPTER VIII

FELICITY AND HER CLIENTS

When Felicity woke up in her enormous, over-draped, over-decorated, gilded, carved, and curved bed she was immediately as wide awake as though she had been up several hours.

There was no slow rousing to the realities of life, no sleepy yawning or languid return from a land of dreams. She dashed the hair out of her eyes, at once put on her glasses (for in private she was short-sighted), and began immediately and systematically to tell her fortune by cards. She did this regularly every morning. It was a preliminary to her day's campaign, when Everett came in with the tea and letters, drew aside the heavy blue curtains, embroidered all over with gold fleur-de-lys, and let in a ray of April sunshine. According to her usual practice, Felicity kept up a running commentary on her correspondence.

"From darling Chetwode.—'My own beautiful little angel, It is quite'—what's this? hop-picking? no—'heart-breaking that I can't get back to you for another week. Tobacco Trust was beaten by a short head, as of course you know, but Onlooker is a dead certainty for to-morrow. Will wire result.

"'I saw a most marvellous old cabinet in a cottage near here'—he *would*—'an extraordinary bargain. It will just go in the corner of——'" She put the four closely written sheets down and opened some more envelopes.

"'Lady Virginia Creeper at home. Five to seven.' Well, I can't help it. Let her stop at home. It's the best place for her.

"'Dearest Lady Chetwode, you haven't forgotten, I am sure, that you promised to see me at three to-morrow. I come to you with my tears. You are the greatest adviser and consoler in all heart troubles. Of late I have been enamoured of sorrow. But for your wonderful "Bureau de Consultation Sentimentale," where should we poor sentimentalists be! Agatha has been simply brutal to me lately. I can find no other word. I look forward to pouring my grief into your shell-like ear. I will bring my new song, "Cruel as the Grave."' How cheering! Jasmyn Vere is perfectly absurd about Agatha. He's a bore, anyhow.

"'Dear old girl; I'm coming to lunch to-day. Everything is rather rotten. I have news of HER. Your aff. brother Savile.'

"'Darling Felicity, be a perfect angel and let my maid see your mauve tea-gown. I know you are so good-natured or I wouldn't dare to ask. I am very anxious about HIM. Oh, why are men always the same? I found out that the wretch instead of being ill, the other day, had taken that awful Lucy Winter to a picture-gallery. What a girl! All red hair and eye-glasses. Let me see you soon. Your devoted friend, Vera Ogilvie.' I am sure Vera needn't worry. Lucy Winter was evidently wild about F. J. Rivers last night. I must tell her. What stupid letters! Oh! here's a new handwriting.

"'98 Half Moon Street, 2 o'clock a.m.—Dear Lady Chetwode, I should be counting the minutes till 4.30, but they pass too slowly to be counted. It's thirteen hours and a half, anyhow. I can't believe I shall really see you again. How eternal yesterday was! Why do the gods follow each feast day with a fast? By the way, I have a little Romney here so marvellously like you that you really ought to see it.'" Felicity smiled. "Steady! Rather a nice handwriting. 'Sincerely yours, Bertie Wilton.' Very promising. 'P.S. I have left a long space between the lines so that you should read between them.' Everett, I'll wear my tailor-made dress this morning and for lunch. The mauve tea-gown at four. I'm only going to the theatre to-night. Let me see, what is it? Oh! the St. James's. The white *crêpe de chine*. Then, remind me to wire to the Creepers on the evening of their afternoon to say I have a chill. Have some gardenias and lilies for the drawing-room, and let me see them. There's the telephone! I suppose Chetwode has rung me up again."

Then followed a one-sided conversation through the telephone, which was fixed by the side of the Louis Quinze bed.

"Yes, darling.... Oh, all right.... Didn't he?... I say, you might come back soon.... I really shouldn't bother about that screen.... What?... I said screen, not scream.... We have heaps more than we want already.... Oh! and ever so many people are coming this afternoon.... A perfectly new young man.... What?... Oh, not bad!... Safety in numbers?... Even if you take the numbers one at a time?... Good-bye."

Savile at lunch was gloomy and taciturn. Absently he had partaken three times of a certain favourite dish, made of chestnuts and cream, repeatedly proffered, with *empressement* and a sort of respectful sympathy, by Greenstock. Then he pushed his plate away, and said when they were alone—

"Funny! I can't eat a thing! Sylvia says I live on nothing but oranges. Pretty rotten sign, eh? Here's what I've heard about HER."

He took out of his purse a neatly-cut-out paragraph from *The Queen*. It stated that Madame Patti had been warmly greeted by all the village of Craig-y-nos, and was about to give an afternoon concert there for the benefit of the poor.

"I shan't have another chance to see HER before I go back," said Savile, looking steadily at his sister.

She followed his idea in a second. "All right! Poor boy! There's no great harm. Shall I give you the—change"—(to Savile, Felicity always spoke of money as change)—"to run up to Wales and hear her sing, and then come back the same evening? It doesn't really matter what time you arrive home, you see. You can stay with me. I'll tell papa you're going to a concert and I want you to stay with me."

Savile was nearly purple with joy. "Would you really? What bricks girls can be!" He shook hands with her with intense self-restraint, and murmured, "I shan't forget this, old girl."

Felicity completed the arrangements, and Savile left, a very happy boy.

At three o'clock Felicity, in her wonderful orchid-mauve tea-gown, was conversing pathetically with Jasmyn Vere, one of the habitués of what her friends called her sentimental bureau.

He was not one of her favourite clients. He was egotistical, and his mania for Agatha was becoming rather a bore. Agatha was a plain, muscular, middle-aged widow who drove him to distraction by her temper and her flirtations. Felicity only stood it at all because he sang and played beautifully, imitated popular actors in his lighter moments, and gave amusing dinners at restaurants.

"What would you have done?" he said. "By mistake, Agatha posted this letter to me!"

He took out of a pale grey morocco case a note with "Stanhope Gate" and a large "A" on it in scarlet and black.

She read—

Dear Bob,

Excuse rush. All rubbish about Jasmin. He's a hopeless idiot, but a good old sort. Mind you fetch me in time for Lingfield Races to-morrow and put me on to a good thing.

Yours,
AGATHA.

Felicity handed it back.

"Just fancy, Lady Chetwode! I confronted her with this. She had put it in the wrong envelope and sent a note meant for me to Captain Henderson. She only roared with laughter. I broke it off finally and she said I should probably break it on again next day."

"And did you?"

"Nothing of the kind. I went away and wrote her a really beautiful letter. I said that I would wipe out the past and begin afresh if she promised never even to recognise Captain Henderson again in the street—or anywhere."

"What did she say, Mr. Vere?"

"Say! She wired 'Sorry imprac.' So it's all over. Now, what do you advise?"

"If you would only leave her alone for about two minutes, she would come round all right; she is so used to you. Or, make her jealous."

"Well, I hope you'll forgive me, but I did try that. In our last interview I said I was coming to see you, and that you were a really womanly woman."

"Oh, thanks very much," said Felicity angrily. "What did she say to that?"

"Laughed that awful laugh of hers, and said I need not worry, as you were very busy."

"She was perfectly right, I am," said Felicity. "Have you left her alone since that?"

"Practically. At least, I only sent her a little thing I thought she'd like."

"A diamond horse-shoe—by any chance?"

"Oh, just a trifle as a souvenir of our long friendship. Then I suggested we should have one final meeting—a *diner d'adieu*."

"And she didn't send the trinket back, and she didn't refuse? Oh, you're all right!"

"I am not all right, dear Lady Chetwode."

"When are you going to see her again?"

"I'm bound to say that I hope to see her next Saturday evening. But just think! She has actually spoken, written of me as a 'hopeless idiot'!"

"Yes. I understood that."

"Should a man forgive such a thing?"

At this stage Felicity's eyes began straying to the clock. "Certainly, if it is true," she said absently.

He left a copy of "Cruel as the Grave" when he went, with many expressions of gratitude, and Felicity said to herself: "What an extraordinary thing! What can he see in Agatha? What can Agatha see in Bob? And there is Vera Ogilvie—really pretty and charming—worrying herself about that dull Captain Henderson, who makes love to every woman he sees, and doesn't care two straws about her." At this point she took up a very handsome photograph of her husband, and looked at it until the tears came into her eyes. It was a charming portrait.

When Bertie Wilton arrived, she brightened up a good deal. He looked better in the afternoon than in the evening, she thought. She liked his bright, intelligent face. And confidences about others do pall after a time. The reaction from Jasmyn made her perhaps more encouraging than she was aware of—she was so depressed about Chetwode's absence. After tea and preliminary platitudes, Mr. Wilton sat beside her on the sofa and took her hand.

"What on earth do you mean by that?" she said, looking more annoyed than surprised.

"You said yourself that life was so short the other night! I haven't the time—I tell you frankly—to be a tame cat and a hanger-on and one of your collection!"

"Really! Sorry you're so busy. I looked upon you as one of the unemployed." She was amazed at his tactlessness.

"You were mistaken. When a thing like this happens—a genuine *coup-de-foudre*—a man is only a fool who doesn't face it and admit it at once. I care for you really, though I haven't known you—very long. I'll cut it out of my life unless you give me ever such a distant hope that you will—like me—too."

"Will you look at my husband's photograph, Mr. Wilton? He's really very handsome—and particularly amusing. We've been married just thirteen months."

"An unlucky number! Yes, I know he's handsome—and, no doubt, delightful. But he isn't here."

"What's that got to do with it?"

"Everything. You know he might be here—with you, and he's not."

"That's his business."

"And mine!" audaciously answered the young man.

"Will you please not take my hand, and recollect that I'm not a housemaid 'walking out' with her young man?"

He did not obey her.

"I should never have suspected you of such bank-holiday manners," she said, at once amused and angry.

"You can call it bank-holiday or anything you like—and if you don't like it I'm sorry, but really you deserve it! You may drive people mad with your little ways, and they may stand it if they like. I can't."

Evidently Mr. Wilton was losing his head. It was quite interesting.

"I saw from the first that firmness is my only chance with you," he said half apologetically. He then made the terrible mistake of trying to kiss her. She slid away like an acrobat, pressed the electric bell, and sat down again with a heightened colour.

"I beg your pardon," said Wilton humbly. "I know it was very wrong. I couldn't help it. You needn't ring and turn me out of the house,—I'll go."

"I wasn't going to."

Greenstock appeared.

"Please bring a glass of iced-water," said Felicity in clear crystal tones.

"Oh, Lady Chetwode!"

During the moment's somewhat awkward interval Felicity stroked up her hair and looked tenderly at Lord Chetwode's photograph.

When the iced-water was brought in he drank it.

She burst out laughing.

"What a penance! Just after tea! Well, I'll forgive you this once only. I think it unspeakable. You're of course very young, so you shall have another chance. You never will be like that again, will you?"

He stood up.

"I never will. I'm very sorry. I quite understand. I can see you are accustomed to invertebrate admirers who spoil you. I made a mistake, because you see I don't happen to be one."

"Chetwode isn't invertebrate!"

Bertie bowed. "Ah, I dare say not. Of that I have no kind of doubt. But you see, he's not here. He's never here. Good-bye."

He took his leave in a very final manner.

Felicity thought over the question with interest. She was sure she would never see Wilton again. Why was Chetwode always away like this? Everybody noticed it.

When Felicity came back from the St. James's Theatre that night she thought that she was a little in love with Bertie Wilton. But she knew she wasn't.

CHAPTER IX

A DINNER AT WILLIS'S

"It seems to me," said Sylvia, "the most unnatural, *treacherous* thing I ever heard of."

She and Woodville were sitting in the library together after breakfast, and he had just told her of Ridokanaki's invitation.

"Besides, I thought you hated him, Frank!"

"If we only dined with people we like, we should practically starve in London."

"But why dine with my enemies?"

"He worships the ground you tread on."

"Then it's all the worse! He wants to spoil our happiness for his own selfish purpose. You know that, and yet you go!"

"Darling, beautiful angel, do let me use my own judgment! I want to hear what he has to say. Don't be angry, Sylvia. I couldn't very well refuse on the ground that he was in love with you, when we—you and I—are not officially—you see, dearest! Of course, it's better I should go."

The door opened slowly and Sir James came in like a procession, and sat down slowly, in his stately, urbane manner.

"Excuse me one moment, Sir James," murmured Woodville, and he collected some papers and vanished. Sylvia waited a few minutes and then rose.

"Don't go, Sylvia," said her father mildly. She stopped. Sylvia was the only person with whom Sir James was never peremptory.

"What has become," he said, a little nervously, though with his usual formality, "of that very sumptuous basket of flowers Mr. Ridokanaki was so kind as to send you?"

"It's in the housekeeper's room, papa." Sylvia's voice to-day was very sweet and high; a sign to those who knew her of some perturbation or cussedness, as Savile used to say.

"Hum! There must be several floral offerings there. To the best of my belief—correct me if I am mistaken—four arrived last week."

"Oh yes, there are *heaps*, papa! It's a perfect garden of flowers."

"So I suppose.... Will you have them brought up to the drawing-room at *once*!—or, when convenient, darling?"

"No, papa. Several are rather faded."

Sir James paused, then with an attempt at calm determination said, with finality—

"If any more arrive, will you recollect, my dear, that I *wish* them to be placed in the drawing-room?"

"Oh, I don't like so many flowers in the drawing-room, papa. But, if you like, I might send them on to one of the hospitals. Perhaps the 'Home of Rest for Chows and Poodles' might——"

"Ridiculous, child! They would not be appreciated there. What do our canine friends care for carnations?" He smiled with satisfaction at the phrase.

In his mind he saw a neat letter to the papers—the sort of thing he dictated to Woodville, and never sent—about "Flowers and Our Four-footed Favourites," signed "Paterfamilias." He was proud of his well-turned phrases, but, though pompous, he was not persistent, and when his secretary had once heard these rigmaroles, and their author had seen them in type—I mean typewriting—Sir James felt for the moment satisfied, and said he had "done a good morning's work."

"I won't have them sent to any hospital, Sylvia. I forbid it."

"Very well, papa. But they're *mine*; surely I can do what I like with them?" she pouted.

"Since they are, as you justly say, my dear, your own personal property, it seems to me only proper that you should write and acknowledge them, thanking the thoughtful sender in an appropriate note."

"But, papa, the thoughtful sender is so *fearfully* floral! I should have to spend nearly all my time writing appropriate notes."

"I don't understand your tone, Sylvia. However, we may let that pass." He opened the newspaper with much rustling and crackling, and said, as if to end the discussion—

"If you receive another basket, or other offering of the same description, from our good friend Ridokanaki, you will write and thank him, will you not?"

"I will not," she answered amiably, as if assenting.

"You *will not*?"

He peered at the modern daughter from behind the *Times*, and recognised in her grey eyes (with as much gratification as such meetings usually afford us) a lifelong friend. It was his own hereditary obstinacy.

Sylvia went to the door, then turned round and said a shade apologetically—

"You see, darling, it seems such a wicked *waste*! Surely the money might be better spent! On—on the unemployed, or something. Why, the other day he sent a thing from Gerard's so enormous that it came quite alone in a van; and another came in a four-wheeler. And I wasn't rude, you know—I kept it."

"I don't quite follow you, my dear. You kept what? The cab?"

"No, the flowers. And I must say it is a pleasure to go and give one's orders now! The kitchen is like a fête at the Botanical Gardens."

Sir James frowned absently, pretending to be suddenly absorbed in the paper until she had gone away, and shut the door. Then he put down the *Times* carefully, and shook with laughter, comfortably to himself, as he only laughed when alone. His daughter's way of receiving homage was very much to his taste.

At the door of the little restaurant in King Street, waiting for him, Woodville found Ridokanaki.

Slight and thin as he was, with his weary, drooping grey moustache, he looked always rather unusual and distinguished. He had black, wrinkled, heavy-lidded eyes, in which Sylvia had discovered a remarkable resemblance to the eyes of a parrot, though the fire in them was very far from being extinguished. He wore a gay light red carnation, but the flowerless Woodville looked far more festive. Woodville's enjoyment of nearly all experiences which were not absolutely depressing was greater than ever since his life of self-repression. To dine alone with the great Ridokanaki on the brink of some kind of sentimental crisis was to him a kind of intellectual, almost a literary joy, one which Sylvia could never either share or understand.

Ridokanaki received him with his most courteous manner. Ridokanaki, like most people, had two remarkably different manners. In society, he had a certain flowery formality, a conventional *empressement*, that, though far from being English, was absolutely different from the geniality of the German, from French tact and bonhomie, and from the Italian grace. It is a manner I have noticed chiefly in Scotchmen and in modern Greeks; its origin is, I fancy, a desire to please, of which the root is pride, not mere amiability or vanity, as in the Latin races. As unfortunately, in Ridokanaki's case, it entirely lacked charm, people simply found him tedious; especially women. On the other hand, in business or, indeed, in anything *really serious*, Ridokanaki was quite royally frank, and natural as a child; considering not at all the feelings of other people and consequently irritating them very little. He had a supreme contempt for petty diplomacy in such matters, regarding it as only worthy of a commercial traveller. His absolute reliability and brutal frankness had made him personally liked in the City, in spite of his phenomenal success—a success that had led to an importance not merely social, but political, and almost historical. Those who saw him in this blunt mood, found him, for the first time, amusing. All really frank people *are* amusing, and would remain so if they could remember that other people may sometimes want to be frank and amusing too.

"There is a subtle difference," remarked Woodville, looking round, "between Willis's and other restaurants. At all others one feels the meal is a means to an end; somehow, here, it seems to be the end itself. Eating is treated as a sacred rite, and in the public preparations of sauces by a head waiter there is something of a religious sacrifice. Look at the waiters, like acolytes, standing round the maitre d'hotel, watching him."

"That's quite true," said Ridokanaki. "You mean people don't dine here for amusement?"

It was not until the coffee and cigar stage was reached that Ridokanaki suddenly said in his *earlier manner*, rather quickly and abruptly: "And why don't you do something better, Mr. Woodville?"

"Could I be doing anything better?" said Woodville, laughing. "I certainly couldn't be dining better."

His host blinked his eyes, waved his hand, and said quickly: "Any one could do what you do for Sir James. It's quite ridiculous, with your brains, that because your uncle didn't leave you a fortune, you should have this absurd career. It isn't a career."

Woodville felt the delightful excitement beginning. To increase it, he reminded himself how Ridokanaki, by a stroke of the pen, could move the fate of nations, and then he turned cold at the thought that Ridokanaki was in love with Sylvia.

"I know," he said, "that I am not doing any good, but I see no prospect of anything better."

Ridokanaki frowned, staring at Woodville rather rudely, and then said: "Of course we're both thinking of the same thing. I mean the same lady."

"Really, Mr. Ridokanaki, I have no idea what you are thinking about. But there is no lady who can possibly concern *our* conversation."

Ridokanaki looked at the clock. It immediately struck ten, tactfully, in a clear subdued tone.

"But"—he spoke rather impatiently—"with all reverence and the most distant respect in the world, there's no reason why I shouldn't speak of the lady. I'm sorry, as you seem to dislike it, but I'm afraid I have no time for fencing now."

Frank was silent.

"Every day," said Ridokanaki in an undertone, "you see that beautiful girl. You live under the same roof. I see her only occasionally, but I understand your feelings." He laughed harshly. "I have the same—as you know."

"Your sentiments, no doubt, do you the greatest possible honour, Mr. Ridokanaki. Mine are those of old friendship."

"Indeed! Well! mine aren't! Can't you see I'm trying to play the game?" He spoke almost coarsely. Woodville liked him better. There was a pause.

"Perhaps," continued the host, "you *think* you only want her friendship, but I don't suppose *she* thinks so. In reality, of course, you want her."

"Really, Mr. Ridokanaki———!"

"Listen, listen! You can't marry her in your present position. I could in mine, but she will never like me while you're there—possibly never. At my best I never had what the French call *le don de plaire aux dames*. Not that age matters, nor ugliness. I haven't the knack. I never had. I bore women. I always did. In that I've always failed, and know it. And it's the only thing I ever cared about. My failure is my tragedy." He smiled. "You have all the advantages on your side, Mr. Woodville. But you're both young, and for that very reason any fancy that may have sprung up *might* be forgotten. With me———"

Woodville looked at him. No, it was not possible to be jealous of his host. Whatever truth there was about his past failure, he could never fascinate Sylvia. She appreciated too fully the plastic side of life; she was a romanticist, and therefore she attached immense importance to the material. (Are not all romantic heroes and heroines beautiful to look at, and always either beautifully or picturesquely dressed?) Sylvia cared far more about her own admiration for a man than for his admiration for her. Homage, except from the *One*, was to her no pleasure, and fortunately she knew exactly what she wanted. Instinctively Woodville knew that she would always love him. Unless, indeed, he should change. But that was impossible. He felt it to be impossible.

So, perhaps, after all, the reports about Ridokanaki's European "successes" were all nonsense. Yes, he had revealed his wound quite openly, and it was a bitter one. He had never been loved "for himself". Woodville pitied him.

"What do you propose?" said Woodville, falling into the Greek's laconic tone.

"Why should a man of your ability go twice a week in an omnibus to a shabby studio, in hopes of making a few pounds a year by copying? Because you're hard up. Why should you be so hard up? I met you once going there, and thought how hard it was. It is dreadful to be hard up.... This is what I propose. I can easily obtain for you a post in connection with my bank. The salary to begin with will be two thousand pounds a year. In Athens."

"Athens!"

"I propose that you try it for a year. During that year I will not see the lady. I will efface myself. If at the end of that time you both still feel the same I shall give up for ever my own wish. You can have a similar post then in London."

"Mr. Ridokanaki, you are too kind. But why, *why* should you?"

"Because I hate to see you near her. If your attachment for each other is the real thing it will stand this separation. Then I shall sink my own feelings. Of course, you see I mean it."

"Thank you," said Woodville, rather touched, and hesitating.

"Please understand," continued Ridokanaki, "that I don't hope for one *moment* there is in any case a chance for me. It's chiefly," he said markedly, "to spare me a year's torture. I can't stand your being in the same house with her. It kills me. I'll try, then, when you've given me this chance, to turn into a friend, a godfather!" He poured out some old brandy and drank it. Woodville changed colour. "They speak of me as a Don Juan, I believe, but I'm really much more of a Don Quixote. If you spare me this year I'll do anything to help you both."

He tapped the liqueur-glass on the table nervously, and went on. "I have got this very badly. Very badly. Oh very."

"*How* can I accept from you———"

"You gain nothing by refusing. The favour is to *me*—remember *that*. In a year you'll be in the position you are now, or worse—if you stay. If you go to Athens you will, of course, have a delightful time. You speak French; you will not have much to do. Only the sort of thing you can do easily and well. Don't you want to see different places, different things?... You are the man I have been looking for. There is some very interesting society in Athens. You would be adored there. But I know that's not what you care about."

"No; I have not the 'true Hellenic spirit.' But I want to be independent. I am afraid I couldn't."

"I shall keep this thing open for a month," said Ridokanaki. "Come and see me. All right.—Yes,—I must go.... You had rather write, not come and see me, eh?"

"You see, I must consult———"

"Of course, you want to consult some one. But, listen. *Don't* go by women! That would be really a pity. They don't know what's good for them." He laughed a little vaguely.

They both stood up.

"Mr. Ridokanaki, you have been more than kind. It is difficult———"

"Well, you'll think it over. Good-bye, Woodville."

Woodville walked away from the restaurant feeling wildly excited. Mr. Ridokanaki made hideous faces in the mirror in his carriage as he drove away and said to himself—

"He thinks I'm the Frog Prince, and he's Prince Charming. Useless! Waste of time! What a fool I am! An evening thrown away! She'll never let him go. He's too good-looking."

I have not given Mr. Ridokanaki's exact words in his soliloquy. This book is intended for general reading.

CHAPTER X

THE THIN END OF THE WEDGE

Felicity was dressing to meet her husband at the station. She tried on three new hats, and finally went back to one that Lord Chetwode had seen before.

"It's too absurd," she said to herself as she drove off. "The extraordinary long time he has been away! Of course I know that nothing but racing or furniture takes him from me. What long letters he writes—he can't be forgetting me! When I see him I never like him to think that I mind. I think a husband ought to have perfect freedom; it's the only way to keep him. It seems to keep him away! Very odd!"

Felicity arrived before the train was due. When it came in and no Chetwode appeared, she blamed the porter and the guard, and asked to see the station-master. He was very charmed with her, but could only patiently repeat that there was not another train that day from the remote little village where Chetwode had gone from Newmarket to pick up an old piece of furniture.

"Really this is too much," said Felicity as she got into the carriage, and with difficulty prevented herself from bursting into tears. "What shall I do? How utterly sickening!" When she got home she found a telegram from Chetwode putting off his return for a day or two, as there was an old dresser in the kitchen of a farmhouse which the owner wouldn't part with, and that he (Chetwode) was not going to lose. It would be a crime to miss it. His telegram (they were always nearly as long as his letters) concluded by saying that, given the information straight from the stables, Peter Pan had a good chance at Sandown.

"Oh!" she said again to herself. "Why, good gracious, I'm miserable! I've put off everything to-day. The worst of it is I can't do anything Chetwode wouldn't like, because he likes everything I do."

She got back into the carriage, and told the coachman to drive to Mrs. Ogilvie's. Poor Vera! She was unhappy too. On her way she met F. J. Rivers walking with the red-haired girl, so she felt sure that Lucy Winter was no longer a thorn in the flesh to Vera. And possibly Vera was very happy to-day! So Felicity wasn't in the mood for her.

She drove to the Park instead (she had put aside all engagements because Chetwode was coming home), and was thoughtful. Suddenly she caught sight of Bertie Wilton chattering to another boy by the railings. He bowed very formally. She stopped the carriage and beckoned to him.

"Would you like to come for a drive?" she said in her sweetest, lowest tone.

"I should like to immensely, as you know only too well, Lady Chetwode, but perhaps I'd better not. My bank-holiday manners might bore you."

"How fickle you are. Come along," she commanded.

He had just been on his way, he said, to an Exhibition of Old Masters to see if there was anything there like the little Romney he had at Half Moon Street that was so like her. So they drove to the New Gallery together.

"I was in the depths of despair when I met you. So much so that I was trying to drown my sorrows in gossip," said Mr. Wilton.

"And I am feeling rather sad," said Felicity; "if we are both horribly depressed perhaps we shall cheer each other up."

"Ah, but I was depressed about you, and you were depressed about some one else. I wonder who it is."

"Guess," she said.

"About some one who isn't here? How extraordinary of him not to be here! Perhaps that's why you like him so much. Perhaps it's very clever—with a person like you—to be never there! Perhaps it's the only way to make you think about him!"

"What do you mean by a person like me?"

"You are right. There is no one like you. Anyhow, it's a cleverness I could never pretend to. I know I should be always there, or thereabouts. At all risks! Yes, all! I always say so."

The New Gallery certainly did seem to raise their spirits. They sat there for a long time exchanging ideas and avoiding the pictures in a marked manner. Felicity had nothing whatever to do that evening, which she had intended to spend with her husband. Savile, who was staying with her, wouldn't be back from Craig-y-nos till heaven knew when. Oddly enough, Mr. Wilton also had no engagement that evening. "So much so," he said, that he had taken a large box at the Gaiety all by himself, to go and see that new thing. Felicity, oddly enough—it was the first night—had not seen the piece. He advised that she should. Then she would have to dine all alone at home while poor Mr. Wilton was going to dine in lonely solemnity at the Carlton. Matters were adjusted so far that she agreed to meet him at the restaurant on condition he made up a party.

"Ask Vera Ogilvie and Captain Henderson. Perhaps the horrid noise and vulgarity, and your society, may brighten me up," she said consolingly, "or at least divert my thoughts."

He sincerely hoped so. Much telephoning at the Club resulted in a promise from Bob and Mrs. Ogilvie to come too, so all was well.

But Felicity dressed for dinner in quite an irritable frame of mind, and nearly cried because she accidentally broke a fan Chetwode had given her.

Mr. Wilton could not have been quite so depressed, really, for after flying off in the adored motor to the Gaiety and the Carlton on urgent matters of business, he went home and looked a very long time at the little Romney quite cheerfully. He found himself beaming so markedly in the mirror over his button-hole and white waistcoat when dressing, that it suddenly struck him both the smile and the button-hole were overdone. They were triumphant, and triumph was vulgar (and premature). He removed them both, and went out with a suitable tinge of gentle restrained melancholy, at once very becoming, respectful, and, he trusted, interesting. He knew he had not lost much ground by his boldness at his first visit. A woman can pardon a moment of audacity more easily than a moment of misplaced respectful coldness. The one may be an attack on her dignity, but the other is a slight to her charm. And Felicity had such pretty manners; there was a touch of formality always with all her gaiety that left a dashing young man in doubt. It was certainly an interesting doubt.

"I never met any one quite so definite in my life as that young man," said Felicity as she ate her toast, holding the *Daily Mail* upside down. She and Savile were sitting rather late over a somewhat silent breakfast. He appeared rather absent-minded and replied to her remark.

"Yes, she was perfectly gorgeous, she looked magnificent. (Pass me the toast, old girl. Thanks.) I say, she looked at me!"

"He said such peculiar things. He's different from other people, certainly," said Felicity argumentatively. "A really brilliant talker. It's so rare."

"No wonder she was called the Nightingale! Thanks very much. Don't talk to me about Jenny Lind."

"I wasn't. You see he's rather lonely and unhappy, after all, you know, under all that cynicism and rattling. Every one has two sides to their character (I believe in Browning up to a certain point)—one to face the world with, and the other to show."

"As to Clara Butt, or any of these newfangled people, that's all rot! I tell you straight, I don't believe it," said Savile.

"You're quite right, dear. One can't deny that he's amusing. There's something so ready about him, and he's so kind and good-hearted as well as clever. He has personality. That's the word."

"Yes, she's a ripping, glorious creature! Oh, it is a pity she married again before I knew her! And a Swede too! But still, that's her business...."

"Of course I told him not to call again until I wrote. There's a good deal in him—when you know him better, you know."

Suddenly Savile looked up and said—

"I say, Felicity, what are you doing to-night?"

"I don't know, I haven't thought of it."

"Chetwode not turning up yesterday you were disappointed."

"I know I was. And, yet—look at this letter!" she showed him another of her husband's long elaborate love-letters.

"Letters are all right, and of course no man, especially your husband, would write all that stuff—I beg your pardon—unless everything was all right. But Chetwode's eccentric."

"I suppose he is. I think I shall dine out to-night, Savile, after all."

"After all what?" asked Savile.

"I'm engaged to-night, dear."

"You're surely not going to dine with Mrs. Ogilvie and her pals—and Wilton, at the Carlton again?"

"How right you are! Clever boy! I'm not, we're going to the Savoy."

"Same idea. Look here, Felicity, you're a bit off colour. It's about Chetwode. He doesn't know it. He ought to."

"Somehow I can't tell him I hate his being away. When he's here there's no need. Besides it's pride, or the family obstinacy."

"Look here, if I could go to Wales for myself, I can go to—what's the name of the place—for you. I'll go off this morning, and pretend I've come to help Chetwode to dig up old cabinets and things. I'll bring him back, give him a hint that people talk. Oh, I know how to do it—and there you are."

"My dear boy, how sweet of you! But it must come from yourself, mind. Perhaps you'd better not. Then I shall see him to-night? You'll bring him."

"I'll undertake to—if you'll give up your Savoy."

Felicity hesitated. "I'll ask them to dine here. I should be too nervous alone. Then you will just come in with Chetwode as early as you can this evening!" (She clapped her hands.) "This evening, won't you? He'll be at the village this afternoon, you know. He says he'll return to-morrow."

"And to-morrow he'll go straight on to York for the races. He only puts it off because he doesn't know you want him. My dear old girl, this has got to be put straight. Now, then, shut up, Felicity!"

"But, Savile, darling—pet! Suppose———"

"Pass me the Bradshaw!"

Felicity made no objection. He again started off for a long and tedious journey. He was supported by the feeling he was doing the right thing, and by re-reading the programme of the Craig-y-nos concert and remembering the look he firmly believed SHE had given him.

Felicity, after telegraphing to Bertie Wilton—"Come to dine here to-night. Can't go out. Felicity Chetwode"—then went to Onslow Square, where she found Sylvia in the garden. Sylvia was not reading a book, and seemed very busy smiling—smiling to herself in a dream of some rose-coloured happiness.

They interchanged ideas without words for a time. Then Sylvia said, "I do hope, Felicity, that Chetwode———"

"He's coming back to-night," she answered decidedly; then said rather abruptly—

"How's Mr. Woodville?"

For the first time Sylvia blushed at his name, as she bent down to pick up the book she had dropped.

"Oh, all right, I suppose. Won't it be nice when we go on the river? We're going quite early—in July."

"Is papa going to have the same house he had last year?"

"Oh, yes; but he's having it all differently furnished. He means to buy it, I think. And I'm to have a music-room opening out of my bedroom, in pale green! Won't it be lovely?"

"Yes," said Felicity, "lovely. And ... what did you say you thought of Bertie Wilton? There's something I rather like about his face."

"Yes, I know what it is—he's very good-looking. Not only that, he might be—well, rather too much of a good thing, if you know what I mean. I wouldn't flirt with him, Felicity."

"I know you wouldn't, darling." Felicity smiled.

"You don't really, I know! It's only fun. Besides, people only love once. You would never care for any one but Chetwode."

"Care! I should think not. But Bertie Wilton's amusing. And he knows simply everything. He's a perfectly brilliant gossip. What do you think is the latest thing about the Valettas and Guy Scott?"

Mrs. Ogilvie and Bob preferred the restaurant; Wilton accepted by telephone, telegraphing afterwards to know if it was all right. A *tête-à-tête* dinner on so short an acquaintance with the most fascinating of hostesses seemed to him almost too great a privilege to be real. Afterwards she told his fortune by cards and he told hers by palmistry.

"You don't tell me all," she said.

"If I told you all—all you are to me—I suppose you would ring for a glass of iced-water again?" said he.

"Oh, no, I shouldn't. I am in a very good temper to-night," said Felicity, laughing.

She had a telegram announcing Chetwode's arrival by the 9.15. She had not mentioned it.

Bertie Wilton looked at her. She seemed rather nervous. He persuaded himself not to go too far again, but it was really rather wonderful that she had, after the iced-water incident, asked him to spend the evening with her.

They had music. He had a voice, a way of singing, and a choice of songs that had often been most useful to him in the beginning of his social and sentimental career. But he was surprised to see that while he was singing something about "my dream, my desire, my despair" she was standing in front of the looking-glass making play with a powder-puff as if he wasn't present, and then appeared to be listening at the door.

He came from the piano and she thanked him with an absent-minded warmth.

Incautiously he said, "It's just what you are, 'My dream.' Will you tell me something? But I shall be in disgrace if I ask."

"What is it?"

"Will you always be my despair?"

"Oh no; oh yes—I mean." Then she said, "There he is!"

There was a sound of cabs outside. Then the door opened and Savile came in, while a voice outside with a slight drawl said, "Where are you, Felicity?"

Felicity ran out of the room and shut the door.

"Extraordinary weather for the time of year," remarked Savile, with a condescending air of putting Wilton at his ease. The young man was smiling, rather uncomfortably for him.

"Very," he answered. "No, thanks," to Savile's hospitable offer of a cigarette. "You've been travelling. How delightful."

"I've just come back with Chetwode from Yorkshire. By the way, you'll excuse my sister for a few minutes. You know what these newly married couples are!"

Bertie Wilton rose.

"Do I not? I should be more than grieved to intrude on anything so sacred as a—shall I say—a home chat? Thanks very much. No, I won't stay now. Ask Lady Chetwode to excuse me. I shall hope to have the pleasure of meeting your brother-in-law here some time quite soon."

He took his leave very cordially, with his usual smiling courtesy, Savile making no effort to detain him, and chuckling a little to himself as he tried to fancy the language Wilton would probably use in the cab on his way home. Then the boy, saying "Well, I've made that all right!" went back to Onslow square.

CHAPTER XI

SAVILE AND SYLVIA

One gay irresponsible April afternoon Sir James and Woodville had gone to the House, and Savile, thinking he might be useful as an escort, strolled into Sylvia's boudoir. It was her favourite room, where she received her intimate friends, played and sang, wrote letters, read novels and poetry, and thought about Woodville. The scent from the lilac in the vases seemed to harmonise with the chintz furniture, covered with a design of large pink rosebuds and vivid green trellis-work; there was a mandoline on the lacquered piano and old coloured prints on the walls; books and music were scattered about in dainty disorder. Sylvia was sitting on the sofa with her pretty fair head bent down and turned away. She did not move when Savile came in, and he was shocked to see she was crying.

Savile turned quite pale with horror. Young as he was, nature and training had made all outward manifestations of emotion so contrary to his traditions and mode of life, and it seemed so unlike Sylvia, that he felt a kind of shame even more strongly than sympathy. He shut the door quietly, whistled to show he was there, and walked slowly up and down the room. Then he stood by the latticed window, looking out, and tried to think of something to say. What comforted girls when they cried? The inspiration "Tea" suggested itself, but that would mean the entrance of outsiders. Presently he said shyly and sympathetically, "Shall I smoke, Sylvia?"

She made a gesture signifying that nothing mattered now, and went on crying.

"I say," said Savile, striking a match, "it can't be as bad as all that."

He went up to the sofa and she held out her hand. Demonstrations of sentiment made him acutely uncomfortable. He put the pretty hand back carefully, and said in a level tone, "I tell you what I should do if I were you. I should tell some one about it—Me, for instance. I've been through a lot—more than any one knows." (Here he gave what he believed to be a bitter smile.) "I might be some use; I'd do my best, anyway."

"Darling boy!"

"Oh, buck up, Sylvia! You're going to tell me every word about it, and more, once you start! I'll help you to start." He waited a moment and then said rather loudly and sternly, "What's wrong between you and Woodville?"

Sylvia sat up, took her handkerchief from her eyes, and stared at him.

"What? Have you guessed?"

"Have I guessed! If I'm always as sharp as this I shall cut myself some day," said the schoolboy ironically. "Why, what do you take me for? Do I live here? Do I come down to breakfast? Aren't I and Woodville great friends? Have I guessed?" He sighed in despair at her denseness.

"Dear boy, I'm sure I'd tell you anything. You're so wonderful and so clever, but how could I know you'd be so sweet about it? Why papa said even you wanted me to marry Mr. Ridokanaki. He quoted you."

"Well, why shouldn't he? I do wish it."

Sylvia's eyes blazed, and she tapped her foot on the carpet.

"Oh, do you? Very well, I'm sure I don't mind! You see it doesn't matter in the very least what you think. After all you're only a little boy."

Savile smiled with genuine amusement, patted her golden hair paternally, and said "Of course. But if I'd happened to suggest your going to the registry office with Woodville this afternoon (I believe there's one somewhere in Kensington, near the work-house), I suppose I'd have been what you call a *dear* little boy, and you'd have let me have some jam for tea.... Poor girl! You must be bad." He laughed, and then said quietly, "Now, then, go ahead."

"Well, Savile, it's too dreadful, and I *will* confide in you. Last night"—Sylvia began talking very volubly—"that horrid old brute—you know, the Greek—asked Frank, Mr. Woodville, to dinner, and actually had the impertinence to offer him a sort of post in a bank, starting at £2000 a year, at Athens. ATHENS! Do you hear? It's in Greece."

"Don't rub it in. This is no time for geography. What else?"

"Well, it was on these conditions. Frank was to go for a year, and all that time the *fiend* has given word of honour never to come and see me, or anything, and if at the end of the year Frank and I are still both the same, *he* will give it up—about me, I mean—and get Frank the same sort of berth in London. And if we're not—just fancy making such a horrible proposition! At Willis's, too!"

"Well, what's the matter with Willis's? Would it have been all right at the 'Cheshire Cheese'?"

"What's the 'Cheshire Cheese'?"

"Never mind," said Savile mysteriously. (He didn't know.) "And if you're *not* still the same?"

"Oh, *then*"—she began to cry again—"of course the wretch thinks there might be a chance for him. He *must* be mad, mustn't he? But the horrible part is that Frank actually thinks of *going*! Fancy! How *degrading*! To accept a favour from my enemy! Isn't Ridokanaki exactly like Machiavelli?"

"Mac who? I see nothing Scotch in the offer. But if he were the living image of Robert Bruce or Robinson Crusoe, that's not the point. Now let's have it straight. Would you marry him in any case?"

"Absolutely never," flashed Sylvia, showing all the celebrated family obstinacy by her beautiful set mouth, "I'd rather——"

"Never mind what you'd rather. *I know* what you'd rather, thanks very much. All right, you mean it. Cross him out. And now we know where we are."

"But still I'm afraid ... you don't seem to think I ought to marry Mr. Woodville, do you?"

"Not that exactly," said Savile. "But I think the man who's been making love to my sister ought to marry *her*. What's more, he's got to."

"Oh, Savile, how can you! Don't you think he cares for me?"

"Off the rails as usual! Yes, I do think so, but it doesn't matter a straw what my thoughts are. It matters what's going to be done."

"But what can be done? Unless he goes away to Athens, I mean."

"Great Scott!" exclaimed Savile, starting up. "What's the use of all his friends—Chetwode, and Mervyn, and Wilton, Vere and Broughton, and heaps more—if they can't get him something? A splendid chap like old Woodville! He was looked upon as a brilliant man at Balliol. I happen to know that—never mind how."

She kissed him. "Do you think, then, that Arthur Mervyn would help him? I mean, do you think that Frank might go on the stage?"

He looked at her quite anxiously, as though he thought her troubles had turned her brain.

"Go on the *stage*! Go on *what* stage? Oh, you'd like to see your husband prancing about like a painted mountebank with a chorus of leading ladies, would you?"

"Oh no, indeed I shouldn't! But are leading ladies all dreadful? And I thought you were in love with a singer yourself," said Sylvia.

Savile threw away his cigarette, with what he hoped was a hollow laugh.

"My dear child, what I choose to do and what I allow my sister to do are two very different things."

"I dare say they are, darling," said Sylvia mildly. "And, *please* don't imagine for one moment that I suppose you ever do anything at all—I mean, that you oughtn't."

"No, I shouldn't worry about *me*," said Savile. "We're talking about *your* troubles.... As if Woodville were such an ass! Catch him going in for such rot!" He laughed. "Sylvia, do you suppose that he's stayed here in this hole," said Savile in a muffled undertone, looking round the exquisite room, and then repeating loudly and defiantly, "I say, in this *Hole*, except for you? Do you think he can't do anything better? Mind you, the Governor's fond of Woodville, it's only the cash and all that. If that idiot of an uncle of his hadn't married his housekeeper, it would have been all right."

"Oh, Savile, fancy, I saw her once! She wore———"

"Describe her dress some other day, dear, for Heaven's sake. What I say is that Woodville is the sort of man who could make his mark."

"Do you think he could make a name by painting?" she asked eagerly.

Savile looked rather sick, and said with patient resignation, "By painting what? The front of the house? Look here, *some one's* got to talk sense. Leave this to me." He then waited a minute, and said, "*I'll* get him something to do!"

"Oh, Savile!—Angel!—Genius! How?"

"Would you mind, very kindly, telling me what Chetwode's our brother-in-law for?" said Savile. "What use is he? When's he ever seen with Felicity? He can't live at curiosity shops and race-meetings. He can't expect to. Why (keep this to yourself) I brought him back last night from Yorkshire! Just in time, don't you know. Felicity was as pleased as Punch."

"My darling boy, I *know* you're sweet and clever, but you talk as if you had any amount of power and influence, and all that!"

"Well, I got Bertie Wilton a decoration!" He laughed. "The Order of the Boot! Now, Sylvia, pull yourself together and I'll see it through. Don't say a word to Woodville, mind that!"

"I adore you for this, Savile." During the interview the girl of twenty seemed to have grown much younger and more inexperienced, and the boy four years her junior, to have become a man.

"Tell me," she asked anxiously, "then am I to pretend to consent to his going to Athens? Why, if he did *go*, well, it would kill me—to begin with!"

"And what to go on with? Rot! It wouldn't kill you. It might spoil your looks, or give you a different sort of looks, that mightn't suit you so well. Awfully jolly it would be, too, having an anxious sister looking out for the post. Thanks! What a life for me! How soon has he to give an answer?"

"Oh, in a month," she answered.

"Well, let things slide; let them remain in ... what's that word?"

"I don't know. In doubt? In ... Chancery?"

"Chancery! Really, Sylvia! I know! In abeyance, that's the word," said Savile. He seemed to take special pleasure in it. "Yes, *abeyance*," he repeated, with a smile. "Well, good-bye! I'm going out." He looked to see that his trousers were turned up and the last button of his waistcoat left unfastened in the correct Eton fashion, and said, "Do look all right in our box to-night, Sylvia. You can if you like, you know."

"I *promise*, Savile! I'd do *anything* for you! I shall never forget."

"You know, looking decent can't do any harm anyway anyhow, to anybody. Never be seen out of uniform." He stopped at the door to say very kindly, "Buck up, dear, and don't go confiding in people—I know what girls are. I suppose now," remarked Savile sarcastically, "that you want a powder-puff, and a cup of tea. I'll tell Price—about the tea, I mean."

CHAPTER XII

AT THE STUDIO

Woodville let himself in with the key, and sat down, in deep despondency, in front of his easel. On it was a second copy of a copy that some one had found him doing at the National Gallery of the great Leonardo. It was not good, and it made him sick to look at it. The studio was a battered little barn in the depths of Chelsea, with the usual dull scent of stale paint and staler tobacco, and very little else; it was quite devoid of the ordinary artistic trappings. From the window shrill cries were heard from the ragged children, who fought and played in the gutter of a sordid street. Woodville had come here to think.

He knew how shocked and distressed Sylvia had been when he had ventured to say that he thought he saw something in the Athenian scheme. He smiled with a slight reaction of gaiety at his surroundings, and wondered, for the hundredth time, why that extraordinary old American lady at the National Gallery had actually ordered from him the second copy of his picture. How marvellously bad it was!

An unusual noise in the street—that of a hansom cab rattling up to the door—startled him. He went to the window, with a strange feeling at his heart. It was impossible that it could be Sylvia; she did not even know the address. It was Sylvia, in pale grey, gracefully paying the cabman while dirty children collected round her feet. He saw through the window that she smiled at them, and gave them a bunch of violets and some money, for which they fought. Horrified, he almost fell down the stairs and opened the door. There was no one else in the house.

She followed him up to the studio, looking pale, but smiling bravely. He closed the door and leant against it. He was panting.

"*What—on—earth*," he said, "do you mean by this madness?"

Sylvia, seeing he was angry, took the hatpin out of her hat, and looked round for a place to sit down and quarrel comfortably.

There was no seat, except a thing that had once been red and once a sofa, but was now a skeleton, and looked so cold and bare that she instinctively took off her chinchilla fur cloak and covered it up. Then she said—

"*Because—I—chose!* I never can get a word with you at home, and I have a perfect right to come and talk to my future husband on a subject that concerns my whole happiness."

She had invented this speech coming along, being prepared for his anger.

"But what would people——"

"People! People! You live for people! Everything matters except me!"

He resolved on calmness.

"Sylvia, dear, since you *are* here," he said quietly, "let us talk reasonably."

He tried to sit next to her, but the sofa gave way, and he found himself kneeling by her side.

They both laughed angrily. He got up and stood by the mantelpiece.

"So you think it is *decent* to accept money to leave the country to please my enemy?" said Sylvia.

"Will you tell me a really better plan by which we can marry in a year on an assured income?" he asked patiently.

"Income! Haven't I when I marry——" But he looked too angry. She changed the sentence and became imploring.

"Frank! If you love me *really*, you can't leave me. Think, every day, every hour without you!"

"Very well! We'll tell your father to-night, and chance it. I won't stand these subterfuges any more. After all, we have the right to do as we like."

"No, Frank, you will *not* tell him till I'm twenty-one. I haven't a right before. You would only be called horrid things—have to go, and—think how mean it is to poor Ridokanaki! Taking his kindness, only to round on him next year! Have you no pride, Frank?"

"Sylvia, that's all very well. But he knows all that. It's his idea."

"Yes, it *would* be! As if I didn't see through his mean, sly scheme. Why, it's not kindness at all!" she exclaimed.

"Good God! Well, what is it? Does he think you'll forget me, do you mean?" said Woodville.

"No, he doesn't. He *knows you'll* forget *me*—in Athens. Oh, Frank," and she suddenly burst out crying, "there'll be Greeks there!"

At the sight of her tears Frank was deeply touched; but he smiled, feeling more in the real world again—the world he knew.

"My dear girl, I don't pretend for one moment to deny that there will be Greeks there. One can't expect the whole country to be expatriated because I go to Athens to work in a bank. What do you want there? Spaniards?"

"Oh! Vulgar taunts and jokes!" She dried her eyes proudly, and then said—

"*Are you sure you'll be true to me?*"

Woodville met unflinchingly that terrible gaze of the inquisitional innocent woman, before which men, guilty or guiltless equally, assume the same self-conscious air of shame. His eyes fell. He had no idea why he felt guilty. Certainly there had never been in his life anything to which Sylvia need have taken exception. Then his spirit asserted itself again.

"Oh, hang it all! I really can't stand this! All right, I won't go. Have it your own way. Distrust me! I dare say you think I deserve it. Is it a pleasure to leave you like this, surrounded by a lot of——Did any one look at you as you came along in the cab?"

"*I* don't know," she said.

He spoke tenderly, passionately now.

"I worship you, Sylvia. You've got that? You take it in?"

"Yes, dearest."

"Well, I'm yours. You can do what you like. I give in. I dare say your woman's instinct is right. And, besides, I can't leave you. And now, my darling, lovely, exquisite angel you will go—AT ONCE!"

"Oh, Frank, forgive me."

A violently loud knock startled them from each other's arms. There was another cab at the door.

"Keep still. Keep over here, Sylvia," commanded Woodville.

From the window he saw, standing on the steps, Savile, in his Eton suit. He smiled and waved his hand to the boy.

"It's Savile. I'll open the door. It'll be all right. I expect he followed you."

In two seconds Sylvia was composed and calm, looking round at the pictures in her chinchilla cloak.

Savile followed his host up, laughing vaguely, and said when he saw Sylvia, in a rather marked way—

"Ah! You didn't believe me when I told you I'd come and fetch you! But, you see, here I am."

"Sweet of you, dear," said Sylvia.

"And a fine place it is—well worth coming to see, isn't it?" said Frank, laughing a great deal.

"Well, we'd better be off. I kept the cab because of dining at Aunt William's to-night. You know, Sylvia, we're late."

"Oh, yes, dear. I'd almost given you up."

As they went to the door, Savile suddenly turned round, and having decided a debate in his mind, said—

"I know all about it. I congratulate you, Woodville. But we'll keep it dark a bit yet, eh?"

Savile thought his knowing of the engagement made it more conventional.

The brother and sister drove off.

Sylvia was silent. Savile did not say a single word until they nearly reached home. Then he remarked casually—

"As I found out where you'd gone, I thought it would sort of look better, eh, for me to fetch you? Didn't mean to be a bore or anything."

"Oh, Savile dear, *thank* you! I'll never——"

"Yes; it's not going to happen again. Go and dress, old girl. Wear your pink. Motor'll be round in half an hour; heaps of time. I'm going too, you know—at Aunt William's."

CHAPTER XIII

AT MRS. OGILVIE'S

"I know what's the matter with you, Vera," said Felicity decidedly, as she sat down in her friend's flat in Cadogan Place. "It's that you haven't got the personal note!"

"I?" said Vera indignantly.

Mrs. Ogilvie was a very pretty dark woman of about thirty, who minimised her good looks and added to her apparent age by dressing in the style which had always suited her. Her dainty drawing-rooms were curiously conventional—the natural result of *carte-blanche* to a fashionable upholsterer. She wore a blue-green Empire tea-gown, a long chain of uncut turquoises, a scarab ring, and a curious comb in her black, loose hair, and was always trying, and always trying in vain, to be unusual. Her name was Lucy (as any one who understood the subject of names must have seen at a glance), but she had changed it to Vera, on the ground that it was more Russian. There seemed no special object in this, as she had married a Scotchman. One really rare possession she certainly had—a husband who, notwithstanding that he felt a mild dislike for her merely, bullied her and interfered with her quite as much as if he were wildly in love. He was a rising barrister, and nearly every evening Vera had to undergo a very cross examination as to what she had done during the day, while being only too well aware that he neither listened to her answers, nor would have been interested if he had.

She sought compensation by being in a continual state of vague enthusiasm about some one or other, invariably choosing for the god of her idolatry some young man who, for one reason or another, could not possibly respond in any way. Yet she was always very much admired, except by the objects of her own Platonic admiration. This gave a certain interest to her life; and her other great pleasure was worshipping and confiding in her friend Felicity.

"Not the personal note!" repeated Mrs. Ogilvie, as if amazed. "I? I'm nothing if not original! Why, I actually copied that extraordinary gown we saw at the Gymnase when we were in Paris, and I wore it last night. It was a good deal noticed too———"

"Oh, yes, you wore it; but you'd copied it. That's just the point," said Felicity. "You can't become original by imitating some one else's peculiarities. The only way to be really unusual is to be oneself—which hardly anybody is. I can't see, though, why on earth you should wish it. It's much nicer to be like everybody else, I think."

"Oh, that you can know from hearsay only, dear," said Vera. "Your husband's come back, hasn't he?" she added irrelevantly.

"Yes. Now, there *is* an unusual man, if you like!" said Felicity. "He has no pose of any sort or kind, and he hasn't the ordinary standard about anything in any way, but likes people really and genuinely on their *own* merits—as he likes things—not because they're cheap or dear!"

"It seems to me so extraordinary that a racing man who is more or less of a sportsman should think little ornaments matter so much! I mean, should worry about china, and so on."

"It is hereditary, dear," said Felicity calmly. "One of his ancestors was a great collector, and the other wasn't—I forget what he was. I *think* a friend of James I, or something military of that sort."

"I'm afraid Chetwode's rather a gambler—that's the only thing that worries me for *you*, dear," said Vera.

"What do you mean by that?" said Felicity.

"Well ... I mean I shouldn't mind my husband attending sales and bringing home a lot of useless beautiful things.... At Christie's you know where you are to a certain extent ... but at Newmarket you don't."

"Chetwode," said Felicity, "isn't a gambler in the ordinary sense. He never plays cards. Little pictures on paste-board fidget him, he says; he loathes Monte Carlo because it's vulgar, and he dislikes roulette and bridge. He's only a gambler in the best sense of the word—and that's a very fine sense!"

"Oh dear, you *are* so clever, Felicity! What *do* you mean?"

"Isn't every one worth anything more or less of a gambler? Isn't going to a dinner-party a risk—that you may be bored? Isn't marriage a lottery—and all that sort of thing? Chetwode is prepared to take risks. That's what I admire about him!"

"He certainly stays away a great deal," said Vera.

"Now, you're only pretending to be disagreeable. You don't mean it. He has just been explaining to me that he hates the sort of things that amuse *me*,—dances and the opera, and social things. Why, then, should he go with me? He does sometimes, but I know it's an agonising sacrifice. What do you think he is going to do to-night? A really rather dreadful thing."

"*I* don't know."

"Dine with me at Aunt William's! A sort of family dinner. Aunt William has asked papa, Sylvia, Savile, and us, and I know just the sort of thing it will be. She has got some excellent match to take Sylvia to dinner, a boring married man for *me*, a suitable old widow or married man's wife for papa, Dolly Clive for Savile (although she isn't out—but then I suppose HE isn't out either, but she spoils Savile), and probably Chetwode will take HER in. Fairly horrible, isn't it? And you know the house. Wax flowers under glass, rep curtains. And the decorations on the table! A strip of looking-glass, surrounded by smilax! And the dinner! Twelve courses, port and sherry—all the fashions of 1860, or a little later, which is worse. Not mahogany and walnuts. Almonds and raisins."

"How is it that you're not ill, and unable to go?" said Vera, looking really concerned, and almost anxious.

"Because I happen to know that she has asked two or three people to come in in the evening. Bertie Wilton is one. He amuses her."

"Bertie Wilton?" exclaimed Vera.

"Yes. He's so clever and persevering! He's been making up steadily to Aunt William for several days, so that she might ask him to meet me. At last she has. As he says, everything comes to the man who won't wait."

"I wonder she approves of him."

"Well, she does in a sort of peculiar way, because he's of a good old family, and hasn't gone into anything—like stockbroking or business of any kind, and she thinks she can find him a nice suitable wife. She thinks Lucy Winter would be very suitable. Aunt William lives for suitability, you know. Isn't it funny of her?"

Vera laughed. "Lucy? Why, I took him with Lucy and me to choose a hat, and there wasn't a thing she could wear. They don't get on at all. Lucy likes serious, intellectual men; she says Bertie's frothy and trivial. She wants to marry a great author, or a politician. However, thank goodness, she's left off bothering about Bobby Henderson." Here Vera sighed heavily.

"Has Bobby left off bothering about Agatha? That's the point."

"*I* don't know," said Vera. "I don't understand him; we've been having some very curious scenes together lately. I can't think what he means."

"He doesn't mean anything at all," said Felicity "and that's what you *won't* understand. What curious things, as you call them, has he been doing lately?"

"Well, he called yesterday by appointment."

"*Your* appointment, I suppose?" said Felicity.

"By telephone," said Vera evasively. "And stayed two hours. And at last I took a very strong line."

"Oh, good gracious! What were you wearing?"

"My yellow gown—and the amber beads; it was quite late and the lights—pink shades—were turned on—or else it would have been too glaring, you know, dear."

"What was your strong line?" said Felicity.

"I suddenly said to him, like some one in a play, 'Do you dislike me, Captain Henderson?'"

Felicity began to laugh. "What a fine speech! What did he say?"

"He answered, 'If I did, I shouldn't be here.' After that—not directly after—he said, 'You look all right in yellow, Mrs. Ogilvie.' Do you think that shows great admiration—or not?"

"I've heard more passionate declarations," said Felicity impartially. "It's the sort of thing Savile would say to *me*. What else did he talk about?"

"Oh, about horses and things, and the new play at the Gaiety, and then I said, 'It's rather a tragic thing for a woman to say, perhaps, but I'm sure you don't care a bit for me, so perhaps you'd better not call any more.'"

"What on earth did he say to that?" said Felicity.

"I'll tell you the exact truth, dear," Vera answered. "He got up and walked round the room, and then said, 'I say, would you think it too awful if I asked for a drink?' What do you think that showed?"

"It showed he was thirsty. I don't think he was going to faint away. Still, I suppose he *had* a drink; and—then—what happened?"

"I hardly like to tell you, dear."

"Go on!"

"I pressed him for his real opinion of me quite frankly, and he said: 'Frankly, I think you're a very pretty woman, and very jolly, but aren't you a bit dotty on some subjects?' Of course I was very much hurt, and said, 'Certainly not about *you*!' So then he said, 'For instance, you always write that you have something particular to say to me, but you never say it. I left several important appointments this afternoon to come round, and you don't seem to have any news.' I *had* said it, you see, but he didn't take it in. I was very much offended at his calling me dotty, but he explained afterwards he only meant that I was 'artistic'!"

Felicity went into fits of laughter. "Well, how did it end?"

"I asked him to dinner for next Wednesday, and he said he was going out of town, and didn't know when he would be back. Now tell me, darling Felicity, *do* you think he is going away to—try and conquer his feelings—or anything of that sort? That is what I should like to think," said Vera.

"No," answered Felicity. "Either it was a lie, because your husband bores him and he didn't *want* to come to dinner, or else he's really going to Newmarket, and doesn't know when he'll be back."

"Tell me, Felicity. I can bear it.... Then—he does not care about me, and I ought to cut him out of my life?"

"I think he likes you all right, but I really shouldn't worry about him," said Felicity.

"Then I certainly shan't. I am far too proud! *How* different Bertie Wilton is," she went on. "So amusing, and lively and nice to every one! But *he* is devoted to *you*."

"Oh, you can have him if you like," said Felicity, "and if you can. You wouldn't get on, really. You see, he isn't romantic, like you, and he likes people best who don't run after him."

"Yes, I have often noticed that in people," said Vera thoughtfully. "I'll tell you *some one*, though, who really interests me; that is your friend, Arthur Mervyn, the actor. He has such a wonderful profile."

"Yes—in fact, two. Oh, that reminds me, I came to ask you to come to Madame Tussaud's to-morrow afternoon. We're making up a party to go to the Chamber of Horrors. I'm taking Sylvia and Bertie. But I can't manage Arthur Mervyn and Bertie too,—at least, not at the Waxworks,—so I'm going some other day with him—I mean Arthur."

"Oh, what fun! I should love to come! Thanks, dearest."

"All right. Meet us there at four, and if you ever meet Arthur Mervyn again, *don't* talk about the stage. He hates it."

"What does he like?"

"He's interested in murders, and things of that kind," said Felicity; "or anything cheery, you know, but *not* the theatre."

"Do you think he would come to see me if I asked him?" asked Vera.

"He hates paying visits," said Felicity, and she glanced round the room judicially, "but if you can make him believe that some horrible crime has been acted here,—I must say it doesn't look like it, all pink and white!—then I think he *would* call. Or, if you suggested—just hinted—that you believed the liftman had once been mixed up in some horrible case—I think he likes poisoning or strangling best—then he'd come like a shot!"

Felicity got up laughing.

"I say," she continued as she fastened her white furs, "have you heard the very latest thing about the Valettas and Guy Scott? Bertie's going to tell me all about it to-night; he is the only *really* brilliant gossip I know. He's raised it to such an art that it's no longer gossip: it's modern history and psychology! First he gets his facts right; then he takes a sort of vivid analytical interest in every one—always a humorously sympathetic view, of course—and has so much imagination that he makes you *see* the whole thing!"

"Good gracious! I think I don't care for gossip about other people," said Vera; "I'm sure I shouldn't like that at all. I am really only interested in my own life."

"Then no wonder you find it so difficult to be amused, darling."

They parted, kissing affectionately.

CHAPTER XIV

LORD CHETWODE

"I have to go down to Fulham this morning; don't let me forget it," said Lord Chetwode.

He was sitting in the green library with Felicity, markedly abstaining from the newspapers surrounding him, and reading over an old catalogue. He was a fair, delicate-looking young man of twenty-eight years the amiability of whose expression seemed accentuated by the upward turning of his minute blonde moustache. He had deep blue eyes, rather far apart, regular features, and a full, very high forehead, on which the fair hair was already growing scanty. Tall and slight, he had a rather casual, boyish air, and beautiful but useful-looking white hands, the hands of the artist. His voice and manner had the soft unobtrusive gentleness that comes to those whose ancestors for long years have dared and commanded. In time, when there's nothing more to fight for, the dash naturally dies out.

"My dear boy, why Fulham?" said Felicity, who was sitting at her writing-table not answering letters.

"About that bit of china."

"We don't want any more china, dear."

"It isn't a question of what we want! It is a question of what it would be a crime to miss. Old Staffordshire going for nothing! Really, Felicity!"

Felicity gave up the point. "I see.... How long are you going to stay in London?" she said.

"Well, I was just thinking.... You know, I don't care much about the season."

"You haven't had ten days of it," his wife answered. "Don't you think it looks rather odd always letting me go to dances and things alone?"

"No. Why odd? You like them. I don't."

She looked rather impatient. "Has it ever struck you that I'm—rather young—and not absolutely hideous?"

"Yes, very often," he said smiling. "Don't I show how it strikes me? Why?"

"It's so difficult to say. Don't you see; people try to flirt with me, and that sort of thing."

"Oh yes, they would. Naturally."

"Sometimes," said Felicity, darting a look at him like a needle, "I shouldn't be surprised if people fell in love with me. So there!"

"You couldn't be less surprised than I should," said her husband, rather proudly. "Shows their good taste."

"Well, for instance—you know Bertie Wilton, don't you?"

"Oh yes, I think I've seen him. A boy who rattles about in a staring red motor-car. How any one on earth can stand those things when they can have horses——"

"That's not the point, Chetwode. I think Bertie Wilton is really in love with me. I really do."

Chetwode tried to look interested. "Is he though?"

"Well, I don't like it," she said pettishly.

"Then, don't stand it. But why? Isn't he a nice fellow?"

"Oh yes, he's very *nice*. But he seems to—sort of think you neglect me."

"But other men go away, for months at a time, shooting big game, or anything of that sort. Only shows he doesn't know.... *What* an ass he must be!" Chetwode's voice showed slight irritation.

"No he's not. He was quite disappointed that you came home the other night when Savile went to fetch you. He went away at once."

"Poor chap!—Well, ask him to dinner," relented Chetwode.

She got up and went close to him. "You're hopeless! Chetwode, do you really care for me—or do you like your curiosities and things better?"

Lord Chetwode looked slightly nervous. His one mortal horror was anything that bore the most distant resemblance to a scene.

"My dear child, why, surely you know you are far and away the most beautiful thing *I* am ever likely to have in my collection!" he said, most admiringly.

She turned away. She was terribly hurt; in her heart she had always feared her husband regarded her as a bibelot. The subject was, to her, too painful to discuss further. That he was sure of her—that showed knowledge of her—that she deserved. But he ought to have *minded about little things* as she would. And he ought not always to be satisfied to leave her safe as the gem of the collection—and just come and look at it sometimes.

Chetwode returned to the catalogue, and then said, "Of course you know I'm going to Teignmouth's for a week."

"And you don't want *me* to go?"

"It's a man's party, darling! Only a week."

"But wouldn't you like me to go racing with you sometimes? I would. I should love to."

He looked up lazily. "I don't think a racecourse is the place for a woman. I like you better here. Of course, come if you like. Whenever you like. Would you like to see Princess Ida run?"

"No, thanks.—Shall you be home to lunch?"

"Yes, I dare say I shall. Are you lunching at home?"

"I was going to Vera's, but I'd rather stay at home—for you."

"Oh, don't do that, dear," he said decidedly. "I may look in at White's."

"Well, when shall I see you?"

"Why this evening, of course. Aren't we going to the opera, or something?" he asked.

"Is it great agony for you to sit out Wagner?" She showed real sympathy. "It's Tannhäuser, you know."

"Can't say I'm keen about it," he answered in a depressed voice.

"If you *like*," she said, slightly piqued, "I could easily go with Sylvia and papa."

"All right—or, I know—don't let us go at all!" said Chetwode. He was now in the hall, and she followed him. "Anything I can do for you, darling?" Then he added, "Don't move for a minute!" He was admiring her golden hair against the tapestry, and smiled with the real pride of the *collectionneur*. "Yes, you must really have your portrait painted, Felicity," he said. "Sargent's the man, I think—or—well, we'll talk it over." He went out, and the door banged relentlessly.

Felicity moved back to the library and looked in the little carved silver mirror that lay on the table. She saw tears gradually stealing into her beautiful blue eyes, enlarging them, and she grew so sorry for the lovely little sad face—in fact for herself!—that she hastily put down the looking-glass, ran upstairs, and rang for her maid to dress her to go out.

Chetwode completely failed in his mission, as the china-man, not expecting him to call so soon, had gone out for the day. He strolled down the Brompton Road, stopping from time to time to look at various pretty things in little curiosity shops, and then he thought, as a contrast, he would have a look at the Albert Memorial. But, changing his mind again, he went a little way into Kensington Gardens. Suddenly, he thought he recognised two people, rather beautiful people, who were sitting under a tree, talking together with animation. It was his sister-in-law, Sylvia, with her little dog, and Woodville. Before they saw him, Sylvia got up and walked quickly towards the Row with the dog. Woodville looked after her, and then strolled slowly towards the bridge. How well the sylvan surroundings suited them! Sylvia was a wood nymph in a fashionable dress; Woodville, a faun in Bond Street clothes. Chetwode smiled to himself. Then for a moment he was surprised.... It seemed odd to see the secretary so far from his usual haunts. Why should Sylvia sit in Kensington Gardens with him, and then go on alone to the Row? However, he thought, it wasn't his business. As he walked towards Knightsbridge, it struck him that he would tell Felicity. She would understand, and explain. Then he thought he wouldn't tell Felicity. He had a curious delicate dislike to mentioning anything he had seen accidentally. He would chaff Sylvia about it when he saw her again.... No, he wouldn't; it would be a shame to make a girl uncomfortable. He would mention it to Woodville. Yes, that was it; he would chaff Woodville about it....

Seeing a hansom, he jumped into it and went to the Club. As he drove there he remembered vaguely several little things that he had noticed subconsciously before, and he began to think that probably Woodville and Sylvia were in love with each other. What more natural! In that case one wouldn't talk about it. It might annoy them. There was nothing on earth Lord Chetwode disliked so much as the idea of anything that would annoy any one.

So he never did tell Woodville nor anybody else. When it did not slip his memory, his almost morbid dread of anything disagreeable prevented his mentioning it, and he left London without having spoken of the incident. Probably it was of no importance after all.

At this time Woodville was really miserable. Their position was more difficult than ever. Of course he had kept his word to her, and written to Ridokanaki that he could not accept the offer. They remained privately engaged, and waiting; Savile their only confidant. He had got rid of the little studio, and was half sorry and half relieved not to be able to go there as a retreat. It had some painful but also some exquisite associations. Since he had made the sacrifice of Athens for Sylvia—for it was a sacrifice—he was, of course, more in love with her than before. That quarter of an hour in Kensington Gardens this morning was the only clandestine appointment they had ever made in the course of five years.

How often he remembered the day he had first arrived at the Croftons! Sylvia was fifteen then, and her governess, Miss Dawe, took the place, as far as could be, of her dead mother, chaperoning Felicity and teaching Sylvia. He remembered that it was bitterly cold and snowing hard. As he passed the schoolroom, of which the door was open, to his own room, escorted by the servant, he heard what sounded like a quarrel going on. A poor old man with a battered accordion was making a pathetic noise on the cold pavement.

"You shall *not* do it, Sylvia!" Miss Dawe was speaking authoritatively. "Your father did not give you five pounds to throw away. It isn't the right thing for young ladies to run down to the hall." And Felicity's voice said imperiously, he knew it afterwards, "Quick; ring the bell, and tell Price to give him the money."

While the electric bell was being rung he distinctly heard the window flung wide open, and a soft thud on the pavement. Sylvia had thrown her purse into the street. From his own room next to the schoolroom, he saw the man pick it up and go away. The doors were closed now, but he imagined the governess's anger. The incident had afterwards seemed very characteristic of the two girls, and he often thought of it.... That evening at dinner he met Sylvia for the first time, and he felt now as if he had loved her ever since. But it was not until three years ago, when she was seventeen, that he betrayed himself, by some word or look.... As she grew into a woman she filled his life, became his one joy and torment. On Felicity's wedding-day he had told Sylvia of his love, and they had become engaged. How was it to end?

CHAPTER XV

MADAME TUSSAUD'S

"Savile," said Sylvia, smoothing his tie unnecessarily (a process that he endured like a martyr who had been very well brought up), "Felicity's coming to fetch me to go to Madame Tussaud's this afternoon. Would you like to come too, dear?"

"Who's your party?"

"Frank is going to meet us there, and Mrs. Ogilvie and Bertie Wilton."

"Oh, then, can I bring Dolly Clive?"

"Yes, of course, she's sweet. But—will they let her come?"

"Yes, they will with us. It's good for her history, and she can have a look in at her precious Charles II. What time?"

"Punctually about four," Felicity said. "Don't forget, Savile!"

"Righto! I'll bring Dolly and take her back. I say, shall we have tea there?"

"Of course, if you want to. Why fancy, Frank said it would be the greatest joke to *dine* there! You can, you know, if you like; wouldn't it be fun, and ghastly, with Byron and Peace, and Sir Campbell-Bannerman, and people like that, looking on?"

"No it wouldn't. These ghastly jokes never come off. They last too long. While you're about it, have a good dinner for Heaven's sake. And I dare say the people at the Savoy are quite as bad—if that's all—if you only knew, and more up to date."

"Yes, very likely, and people at real places often have no more expression than the waxworks. But, Savile, I thought it was all off between you and Dolly now?"

He answered, with a sigh, "So it is, in a way, but you'll learn in this life, old girl, that you must take what you can get—especially if you're not sure you can get it! Mind you," lowering his voice, "that little foreign bounder, de Saules, isn't going to have it all his own way."

"Oh," Sylvia, being in good spirits, was inclined to tease him, "I should have thought it would be a capital opportunity to show an intelligent foreigner the sights of London!"

"The intelligent foreigners *are* the sights of London," said Savile as he went out.

The same morning Vera rustled into her friend's room, with her usual air of vagueness and devotion, and said with a sort of despairing cry—

"Oh, Felicity darling! you're the only person in the world who always has clothes for every occasion, and knows everything. How on earth does one dress for Tussaud's? Should you regard it as a Private View, or treat it more like—say—Princes'?"

"Neither. Why on earth Princes'? Were you thinking of bringing your skates?"

"Don't be absurd. Then I had better not wear my new Paquin?"

"Certainly not. Nothing trailing, or showy. But for Heaven's sake don't dress for skating or bicycling. I fancy there is a notice up to say you can't do either of those things there. And please not too much of your Oriental embroideries."

"Well, my new tailor-made dress then, and a large hat?"

Felicity laughed.

"My dear girl, what does it matter? If you fondly imagine that any one will look at your dress while there are *real* horrors to see———!"

"Darling little creature!" said Vera, who absolutely idolised Felicity, and looked up to her in the most absurd way, although she was five years younger—often taking her ironical advice quite literally, and regarding her as a rare combination of faultless angel, brilliant genius, and perfect beauty.

"And now," said Felicity, standing up to her full height—which was far from imposing—"*Go*, please, Vera! I expect the hairdresser."

"Oh, then, you're taking a little trouble, after all," Vera said, laughing, and she vanished vaguely, behind a brocaded *portière*, leaving a very faint perfume of gilliflower.

The party met fairly punctually in the hideous hall, furnished with draughts and red velvet. The gloom was intensified by the sound of an emaciated orchestra playing "She was a Miller's Daughter," with a thin reckless airiness that was almost ghostly.

"Let's be a regular party," said Felicity, "and keep together, and get that nice chasseur-looking person to show us round."

Savile and Dolly preferred to stroll about alone, with a catalogue, and "take the Royal Family in their order." Woodville and Sylvia sat down near the band.

The amiable chasseur, who greatly enjoyed his work, and who saw that the living celebrities left our friends rather cold, showed them "The road to ruing," as displayed in six tableaux.

"No. 1, Temptation. 'Ere you see the young man being tempted to 'is ruing by cards—and what not."

The party gazed at the green table on which were strewn a few cards.

"Fancy being able to be ruined by only half a pack of cards!" said Felicity admiringly.

"Who," asked Wilton with interest, "is the lady in crimson satin, with pearls as big as oysters and diamonds like broken windows, holding out her hand so cordially to welcome the young man with long hair and an intelligent expression? (Obviously a very excellent model of Arthur Symons, the poet)."

"Why, she's the Decoy," said the chasseur, with intense relish. A sinister man with very black hair (probably in collusion with the decoy) was looking on, enjoying the scene.

"How symbolic those two champagne-glasses are on the card-table! What is that dark brown liquid in them?" asked Wilton.

"Still champagne, I suppose," said Felicity.

"Oh dear, yes, ma'am! It ain't been changed. Nothing's been changed."

"How sad it all is!" sighed Vera.

"It gets better later on," said Bertie consolingly.

"No. 3. 'Ere you find 'im ruinged by gambling. Take notice of the evil appearance of 'is accomplice."

The young man was now forging ahead for all he was worth (and a great deal more) with a cheque-book and a fountain pen. The sinister friend was leaning over his shoulder as if to jog his elbow.

"No. 4. 'Ere you see the sad result of all these goings on," said the chasseur morally, if vaguely. "The pore young man is condemned to several years."

"Does he break out again?" asked Wilton.

"Oh, lor', yes, sir! Don't you fret! *he* breaks out again all right. And 'ere you 'ave *Revenge*! A dark resolve 'as taken distinct form in the ruinged man's mind."

"Poor man, how long his hair has grown in prison," murmured Felicity sympathetically. "Who has he killed?"

"Why, the decoy!" said the chasseur, "and (if you ask me) serve 'er right!"

"How helpful all this is," said Bertie Wilton. "I feel really a better man since I've seen it. Seriously, I don't think I shall ever drink champagne of that colour now that we have seen the appalling results. It's a terrible lesson, isn't it, Lady Chetwode?"

They left the young man to his fate and followed the showman.

"'Ere we see Mary Manning, also Frederick George of same name, who, in singularly atrocious circumstances, killed a retired custom-'ouse officer."

"Why?" asked Vera inquisitively.

"They took against him, miss."

"I think I like the ladies best," said Bertie. "Who is this really terrible-looking woman?"

The showman hurried towards him, still repeating like a parrot what he wished to tell them about Manning.

"Yes, Manning was a railway guard, and 'is wife was highly connected with the best families—as lady's-maid. Ah, sir, you're looking at Cathering Webster. She was executed for the murder of another lady at Richmond. Jealousy was the reason of 'er motive for the crime."

"I say," said Felicity suddenly, to the guide, "don't you find all this terribly depressing? Do you hate all these creatures?"

"No, miss," said the showman smilingly, "I'm so used to them. I regard them almost like relations. 'Ere we 'ave a couple of French criminals. *Their* little game, if you please, was to decoy to their 'ome young ladies, and take away all their belongings, and everything else they possessed."

"Oh, how horrid of them!" said Vera indignantly.

The chasseur grinned. "Yes, they weren't nice people, miss."

"I think you would like Burke and Hare, sir," he said persuasively to Wilton. "Let me tell you a bit about them."

"He talks as if they were Marshall and Snelgrove," murmured Wilton.

"What was the reason of their motive?" asked Felicity.

"Strychnine, miss," readily answered the well-informed guide.

"I suppose people get awfully hardened, eventually, to this sort of thing? *I'm* not. I'm terribly nervous. I'm frightened out of my life. If it weren't for you, Lady Chetwode, I should faint, and be carried out by the emergency exit."

While the chasseur went into atrocious details, Bertie was so frightened that he had to hold Felicity's hand.... Vera felt quite out of it, and in the cold.

When once they got into the Chamber of Horrors, nobody had taken any notice of her, nor even heard her remarks. Felicity and Bertie were evidently at once excited and amused. As she was standing alone pretending to look at some relics, the gallant chasseur came up and said, "There's an emergency exit 'ere, if you like to go out 'ere, madam."

"There seems to be nothing else," said Bertie. "As soon as you get into Madame Tussaud's the main object seems to be to drive you out. They keep on telling you *how* you can get out, and *where* you can get out, and when. How wonderful a fire would be here!"

"Do you think Sylvia got out by one of the emergency exits? I haven't seen her or Woodville for some time."

"Oh, can't you let them have tea in peace?" said Bertie.

"I'm sure they are not having tea. Sylvia hates Bath buns. But we'll go and look for them, and the children too."

Savile and Dolly were found on a red velvet sofa, sulking, while Sylvia and Woodville were still listening to the band.

Dolly complained that Savile had been "horrid to her about Charles II," and that he said she was too young to see the Horrors.

Sylvia and Woodville had simply forgotten all about the waxworks.

The band was so very good and had been playing musical-comedy airs so charmingly.

Wilton declared his nerves were completely shattered and he must have a rest cure in the form of being driven home by Felicity, he could not possibly go alone.

Vera had to fetch Mr. Ogilvie from the chambers. Savile, feeling very grown-up, drove Dolly back in a hansom.

"Oughtn't I to take you?" said Felicity to Sylvia.

"My dear Lady Chetwode, please remember that Woodville is staying in the same house as Miss Crofton, and it is perfectly absurd, and cruelty to the horses to drag them out of their way, when you live in Park Street, and I only a stone's-throw from you! *Do* be practical!" cried Wilton.

"Oh, all right."

"Won't you take Miss Sylvia home?" said Bertie.

"Oh, certainly," said Woodville, and they walked a little way towards the cab together.

Ever since Ridokanaki's departure, Woodville, having consented to keep their engagement secret until Sylvia was twenty-one, had sought, and thought he had found, a solution, which was at once balm to his conscience and support to his pride. Sylvia and he should make a compact that they should be to one another in reality as they appeared to her father, and to the world: friends only. They would neither seek nor avoid *tête-a-têtes*, and when alone would ignore, crush, and temporarily forget their tenderer relations. Sylvia had willingly, eagerly agreed. She knew, in fact, that these were the only terms on which he would remain there. And yet it was rather hard. She remembered (how clearly!) that during all these years he had kissed her on seven separate occasions only, and those occasions, after the first, were always, or nearly always, at her suggestion—because it was her birthday—or because it was Christmas Day—because she was unhappy—or because he was in good spirits, and similar reasons. How admirable they had seemed! How sophistically she argued!

All this, Woodville had explained, must now cease. He tried with some difficulty to point out to her that this innovation was because he loved her, not less, but more. He could not trust himself, and did not intend to try. She was so happy to think he had given up going to Athens that she was only too glad to consent to anything.

This was the first time they had been alone since the compact. She looked at him beamingly as they started on their drive.

"But I'm not going home," said Woodville.

"Aren't you? Where are you going?"

"To the Beafsteak Club. I'm dining with Mervyn, and we're not going to dress. I'll take you home first, if you like."

"No," said Sylvia. "I shall drive you nearly as far as the Club, drop you, and then go home by myself." She spoke decidedly, and gave the direction to the cabman. She had calculated that it would be a longer drive.

"It's twice as far!" she said with childish triumph. He looked at her trusting, adoring eyes, her smiling, longing lips, and looked out of the window. She put her hand on his arm, and he moved away quickly, almost shaking her off. With a smile she sat as far from him as possible. They began talking of all kinds of things—Sylvia talked most and most gaily—then, gradually, they fell into silence.

It was the end of a warm April day; they passed quickly, in the jingling cab, through the stale London streets, breathing the spring air that paradoxically suggested country walks, tender vows, sentiment and romance.... Was she hurt at his coldness? On the contrary, it seemed to exhilarate her. So close, yet so absolutely separated—not in mind, but by his will only—by that extraordinary moral sense of his, that was, to her, in her innocence, a dark mystery. Sylvia never forgot that drive. She felt one of those unforgettable moments of exalted passion, like the attainment of some great height that one may never reach again. She worshipped him.

As they reached the end of their drive, the personal magnetism was almost too strong for her—she nearly took his hand again, but resisted. The cab stopped.

"I should like to drive you back, Sylvia," he said, as he got out, "but—it's better not."

"All right!—Good-bye! I suppose I shall see you to-morrow morning."

"I hate leaving you here," he said.

"Never mind!" She smiled brightly, and waved her hand. The cab drove off, and he seemed to be swallowed up by the darkness of the street, looking, as she thought, very wonderful, very handsome.... Then, quite suddenly, she felt cold, quite lonely, almost forsaken....

For hours she could not shake off the horrible impression of his walking away from her into the darkness, leaving her alone.

After her conventional evening at home, she shed bitter tears on her pillow. Could he care for her really? She knew he did, and she suddenly suspected that it was a sort of pleasure, a kind of indulgence to him to play the ascetic when so near her, and at this fancy she felt a little momentary resentment. But as soon as she saw him again, a word or a smile was sunshine and life to her. She wanted so little, and she was again her happy and gentle self.... At least, she could see him—while, if he had gone to Athens.... Surely they would not have to wait a year? No—Savile would find out some splendid arrangement that would make it all right. She loved Woodville too much not to be hopeful; he cared too much for her not to feel, almost, despair. The conditions of their present existence were far harder for him, though she never knew it, and did not dream how much she—not he—was exacting.

CHAPTER XVI

A GOLDEN DAY

Woodville was sitting in the library, supposed to be digging up old Bluebooks for Sir James, but, instead, he found himself lingering over a curious book of poems with a white cover and a black mask on the outside. He read (and sighed):

Dear, were you mine for one full hour,A lifetime, an hour, that is all I ask.Dear, like a thing of lace, or a flowerBefore the end would you drop your mask?

Dear, days and hours are not for me—I may not know you, nor forgive,For you are like the distant sea,And I upon the hills must live.

"This," he said to himself, "is rot for me! It isn't a good poem,—and if it were a good poem (it has *some* good qualities) it's idiotic for me to read poetry. What *is* the matter with me?" He put down all the books, and went and looked at himself in the mirror. He saw a face rather paler, more worn than some weeks ago.

For the last few nights Woodville had suffered from insomnia—a trouble at which he used to scoff and smile, firmly believing, until it had been his own experience, that it was affectation. The second day that he had gone to look out of the window at about five o'clock in the morning, feeling that curious lucid clearness of brain, almost a kind of second-sight, sometimes produced by unwonted sleeplessness, he still thought that people made much too much fuss about a restless night or two.

"Suppose a fellow couldn't sleep for a time! Well, he can read, or work. It was nothing." But, about eleven in the morning the exaltation of the wakefulness had gone off, and he felt stupid and depressed. He suddenly began to feel anxious about himself. Of course, it was all Sylvia! This life, seeing her more or less all day, under the same roof, pretending to be only friends, without any sort of vent, any expression, verbal or otherwise, for his sentiment, was impossible! It was unbearable! He ought to have gone to Athens.... Suddenly Sylvia came into the room. She looked the picture of freshness and happiness. She had come to fetch a book, she said. But she lingered a moment, to ask Woodville if he liked her new dress. It was a Paris marvel of simplicity in pale grey, and neither disguised nor over-emphasised the lines of her exquisite figure.

"Yes, I think it's all right," said Woodville.

"*All right!*" she exclaimed indignantly. "Don't you *see* how it fits? Why, it's simply wonderful! How heartless you are!" There was just a tinge of coquetry in her manner, which was rather unwonted. "You're not looking very well to-day," she said, looking sympathetically at him.

"I'm very well. I'm always all right."

"Are you angry with me, Frank? What's the matter? What's that you're reading?" She snatched the book of poems away from him, read the poem and blushed with pleasure.

"Yes! You see that's what I'm reduced to!" he said.

"Frank, I don't think you go out enough. Look, what a lovely day it is!"

"Where do you propose I should go? To the theatre to-night? I hate theatres." He spoke irritably.

"No," she said in a low, soft voice; "let's break the compact, just for once—*just for once!*" She was instinctively taking advantage of a kind of weakness he showed this morning for the first time—due to his nervous fatigue—the weariness of long self-repression.

"Certainly not!" he answered, with no conviction whatever. "Whose birthday is it? It isn't Christmas Day—it isn't Midsummer Day. No! I don't see any excuse for doing it."

"Yes, there's a reason! It will be Sexagesima Sunday next week!"

"So it will!"

"Ah, you admit that! Well, let's go and have lunch at Richmond—or somewhere like that!"

"My poor dear child, what's the matter! You're not sane.... Besides, it's impossible," said Woodville, hesitating, in a hopeful voice.

"It isn't impossible. Papa's gone out for the whole day. Leave it to me! I'll arrange it. If the worst came to the worst, I could tell papa that I longed for a little air and made you take me down to Richmond! Why! you know he wouldn't mind. He would see nothing in it. We'd be back before five."

Woodville looked tempted.

"Besides, there would *be* nothing in it," added Sylvia softly.

He took her hand. "Temptress!" he said. "Of course there wouldn't be any earthly harm in it," he said doubtfully.

"Then we're going to do it!"

"Are we, Eve?"

"Oh, Frank!" she exclaimed passionately, "it's too absurd, too unnatural! Why shouldn't we have a moment's happiness? Aren't we going to be married next year?"

"Probably, if I live through this one."

She was smiling, for she knew she had won. "Yes, you'll live through it all right—if you only have a little fresh air and change of scene now and then!"

"I couldn't do it, Sylvia!—How should we go?"

"Drive in a hansom?"

"No, I'll meet you at the Underground Railway at Earl's Court."

"When?" she asked.

"In twenty minutes."

"All right. We'll have a holiday! Everybody has a holiday sometimes! It's a heavenly day! We will go and walk in Richmond Park and forget all about the compact worries till we come back at tea-time. Papa won't, then, be back, and no one will ever know anything about it!" She clapped her hands. He smiled at her.

"It's settled," he said.

As she went out of the door, she murmured, "In twenty minutes, then," and vanished, radiant.

When she had gone, he found all trace of his usual scruples had inexplicably disappeared. It was natural, and (he said to himself) it was right! What use was this continual sacrifice of the precious hours and days of their youth—for an Idea? Besides, she looked so lovely. A man must be a stone to refuse such a delightful suggestion, or a fool. He was neither. The reaction was inevitable, and in half an hour they were in the train together, in the highest spirits, all cares thrown aside, in the hope of the spring, of sunlight, fresh air, and above all, being together alone, free, for several hours. It seemed like a dream, a dream with the added substantial tangible joy of being real.

CHAPTER XVII

SAVILE TAKES A LINE

"Hallo, Savile!" said Felicity, who was putting the last touch to her veil in front of the mirror. "Nice boy! You're just what I wanted. Come out with me!"

It was about twelve o'clock, a lovely warm morning. The first hum of the season was just beginning, like the big orchestra of London tuning up. There seemed a sort of suppressed excitement in the air. People of average spirits appeared unusually happy; the very highly strung seemed just a little wild; their eyes dancing, their tread lighter, and laughs were heard on the smallest provocation. Certainly the vision that met Felicity in the mirror was exhilarating enough. Dressed in the softest of blues, with a large brown hat on her golden hair, she looked like a pastel—a combination of the vagueness, remoteness, and delicacy of a Whistler with the concrete piquancy of a sketch in *L'Art et La Mode*.

Savile, however, showed none of the intoxicating effect of a gay London morning. He seemed more serious, more self-controlled, more correct even than usual.

"Where's Chetwode?" he asked.

"Oh, he's just going out, dear, I think. Do you want him? Shall I ring?"

"No; I shouldn't ring. What's the point of that except to delay my seeing him? No; I want to see him, so I'll go and look for him, and perhaps go out with him. I suppose you're driving, and don't need me?"

"*Need* you? Oh no, darling; not exactly. Only I thought it would be fun to go out and look at the people in the Row—and laugh at them. Besides, I always drive down Piccadilly and Bond Street when I have a new hat, to find out whether it suits me. It's such fun. I can always tell."

"Frightfully comic, no doubt, but I've got something more important to think about this morning."

"What a bad temper you're in, Savile! Anything wrong, darling?"

"Just like a girl!" said Savile. "I never *yet* showed any woman I had something to do that she didn't say I was in a bad temper."

Felicity laughed. He went to the door and added—

"Oh, by the way, don't trouble to give my love to Wilton."

She made a rush for him, and he ran out of the room.

He found Lord Chetwode, as usual, in the green library, not reading the newspapers, and reposefully smoking. Savile accepted a cigarette and sat down.

"Thought you were going out?" said Savile.

"Yes, so did I. But why go out? It's all right here. Besides, I *am* going out. No hurry."

"Good," said Savile, and they smoked in silence.

"You're not stopping in town long, are you?" said Savile.

"No, old boy. Season's beginning. I hate London. I'm going week-ending next Saturday."

"And you won't come back?"

"I shall probably stop ten days."

"I've got something to say to you," said Savile.

Lord Chetwode smiled encouragingly.

"Fire away!"

"There's something I want particularly to ask you."

There was a pause. Such a remark as this from any one but Savile would have alarmed Chetwode, suggesting something in the nature of a scene, but he felt pretty safe with his brother-in-law of sixteen. He wondered what on earth the boy wanted, and felt only good-humouredly amused. Savile had chosen his words before he came, and had that rash longing we all feel when we have made out a verbal programme, to make the suitable remark before the occasion arises.

"We're both men of the world," began Savile.

"Are we, though?" said Chetwode. "Please spare me this irony! *You*'re a man of the world all right, I know. *I* don't pretend to be."

"May as well come to the point," said Savile. "You know Woodville, don't you?"

"Woodville? Rather. Capital chap. What's wrong with him?"

"There's nothing wrong with him," said Savile, "but I want to get him something to do."

"Really? Doesn't he like being with you and Sir James and Sylvia, and all that?"

"Yes, he likes it all right. But he isn't much with Sylvia and all that. He'd like to be more. So would she—a good deal more. That's the point."

Chetwode instantly recollected the incident in the Park. He said without turning a hair, "Quite so. Most natural, I'm sure——" and then thought a moment. Savile was silent.

"What Woodville *needs*," said Chetwode, lighting another cigarette, "is, of course, less of you and Sir James, and a great deal more of Sylvia; and he can't very well marry her while he's her father's secretary. Though—by Jove!—I don't see why not!"

"What rot!" said Savile.

"Yes, you're right, Savile. It's true Sir James wouldn't give him a minute's time for anything. Well, you want me to get him something to do then?"

"Now, look here, Chetwode, don't play the fool about this. Here's a chap, considered a brilliant man at Oxford; in every way a thoroughly good sort, and a gentleman, who, if it weren't for circumstances, would have been called a good match."

"If it weren't for circumstances, anybody would be called a good match," said Chetwode casually.

"What sort of thing do you think you can get him?" asked Savile, "before Saturday?"

"Before Saturday? Well, what sort of thing does he want before Saturday?"

"Oh, something political. Or some post—or something diplomatic."

"You're pleased to be vague," said Chetwode, bowing.

"Oh, all right! Then you can't do it?" Savile stood up.

"Please, Savile, no violence! Take another cigarette. Of course, the idea is that I must talk to somebody. Perhaps Teignmouth——"

"Put the whole thing before him," said Savile.

"The beastly part is no one will stand being talked to about things, and everybody hates having the whole matter put before them—unless it's gossip. Then, by Jove, won't they go into details!"

Savile controlled his feelings, and said, "Well, here's a romantic story, a lovely girl—young man disinherited——"

Chetwode visibly shrank from the explicitness.

"All right, old boy. Look here, I see your point—I give you my word I'll try."

Savile, terrified at the thought that he might have been a bore, got up again and held out his hand.

"When will you let me know?"

"As soon as I've seen anybody or done anything that seems to help at all.... Let's see, what's your telephone number?"

"I haven't got any telephone number," said Savile, "at least, not on *this* subject. Won't kill you to wire and let me know when I can see you again."

"Good! that's the idea. And look here, Savile, you think I am not going to trouble, I can see that. But you happen to be wrong. I'll fix it up all right."

"I thought you would," said Savile.

"And we won't talk it over, don't you know, to—a—women or anything. Eh?"

"Catch me," said Savile.

"Well, I must go out now," said Chetwode. "Can I drop you?"

"Think I'll walk," said Savile.

They shook hands most cordially. Chetwode went out smiling to himself, and strolled towards the Club.

CHAPTER XVIII

FELICITY'S ENGAGEMENTS

"Is Lady Chetwode at home?"

Before Greenstock, who seemed about to give a negative answer, could reply, Wilton went on.

"Oh yes, she *must* be at home; please ask her to read this note, and send me down a verbal answer immediately."

"Very well, sir."

"I won't get out, Greenstock. I'll just wait in the motor till I get an answer."

"Yes, sir."

Wilton turned to the chauffeur and said, "How do you think she's looking to-day, Pearce?"

The motor had recently been painted green, because Felicity had said it was too compromising to drive with Wilton in a scarlet one.

"Never better, sir," said the chauffeur.

"You know I *was* right, Pearce. Green suits her much better than scarlet. In fact, I rather doubt whether you could point me out a case in which I am ever wrong, Pearce. With regard to the motor, I mean, of course."

"Oh no, sir."

"How do you mean 'Oh no'? Do you mean I'm ever wrong then?"

"Oh no, sir."

They both looked with suppressed pride at the automobile which was snorting rather impatiently under these personal remarks.

Greenstock appeared.

"Will you step in, sir?"

At the summons Wilton sprang out and ran quickly up into the drawing-room.

It was a beautiful room with hardly anything in it; a large, high, empty room in pure First Empire style. A small yellow sofa with gilded claws, and narrow bolster cushions, was near the fireplace; a light blue curved settee, with animals' heads, was in the middle of the room. There was a highly polished parquet floor with no carpet, a magnificent chandelier, and the curtains were held up by elaborately carved and gilded cornices with warlike ornaments.

Bertie wandered round the room, tried, vainly, to see himself in the narrow looking-glass, which was placed too high, and admired the refreshing absence of fat cushions, unnecessary draperies, photographs, and vases of flowers. On a small console-table was one immense basket of mauve orchids. Bertie was looking at this with some curiosity, not unmixed with annoyance, when Felicity came into the room.

"How *marvellous* of you!" he exclaimed. "Again I'm thunderstruck at your having *exactly* the right thing to wear, to come down early in the morning to see a too persistent friend!" He looked at her dress. "Pale green—how well it suits you; and how wonderful of you to be so empireish—at this hour!"

"What *do* you want, Bertie?" said Felicity, smiling, but impatiently.

"Oh, please don't be so definite! and I thought you knew!"

"Please don't be so imbecile; I don't want to know."

They both sat down, and she held out the letter.

"I didn't read all this," she said; "but you seem to have given me a programme of your engagements for to-day. I can't think why."

"Because I want to know yours. To come to the point," said Wilton. "If I go to the Ogilvies', will you be there?"

"Well, of course! As if Vera could have a musical afternoon without me!"

"Good, that's settled. And what are you doing to-night?"

"Well, which do you advise?" she said. "The Creepers'? Or Jasmyn Vere's party?"

"If I might advise, *do* go there. His things are really rather jolly. Is Chetwode coming?"

"No, Chetwode's struck. He won't go to anything more. He's going away on Saturday for the week end, so I shall stop at home with him to-morrow. To-night I'll go to Jasmyn Vere's. What time does one get there?"

"One gets there a little before you do, for the pleasure of the anxiety and agonising suspense of dreading you won't come and knowing you will." He got up. "If you would turn up at half-past ten—before the crush—we could sort of sit out, and laugh at the people."

"Perhaps I shall," said Felicity.

"Lady Chetwode, you are as good as you are beautiful."

"Oh, don't carry on like that, Bertie! I suppose it's through your having gone to that ball as Louis XIX; every now and then you seem to think you're in the last century."

"But when I'm here, I know I'm in the next," and he took his leave in the highest spirits.

At lunch, "Chetwode," said Felicity, "I shall be at Vera's till seven. They're going to have the wonderful new child harpist. He looks like a sort of cherub, with golden hair."

"Little beast," said Chetwode, "he ought to be in bed."

"Oh, darling, not at four in the afternoon! And what about to-night? I suppose we dine together at home? and then I'm going to Jasmyn Vere's, one of his musical parties."

"Oh, yes."

"Chetwode dear, you know the horses will be out all the afternoon. I thought I'd have the carriage just to *take* me to the party and come home in a cab—it's only round the corner. Is there any off-chance of your coming to fetch me? Oh *do*! You really might!"

"No," said Chetwode. He added, "No doubt Wilton will see you home."

She looked up quickly. Was there a tone of irony in his voice? Could he be a shade jealous? How delightful!

"Why, I can come home alone," she said. "It's not sure that Bertie and I will both want to leave at the same time."

"But I should think it's on the cards," said Chetwode, rather coldly.

"No use bothering you to come?"

"None at all. Who does the hostess at Jasmyn's parties?"

"Oh, Bertie's mother, Lady Nora Wilton, you know."

"I see."

"Did you think," said Felicity, laughing, "that it would be Agatha, Mrs. Wilkinson?"

"Oh—you mean the woman who's so fond of horses. Why, is she a friend of Vere's?"

"Some people say so, of course I don't know."

"I always see her," said Chetwode, "at races, with Bobby Henderson."

"Oh yes," said Felicity, "but that's only intellectual sympathy! I can't see the point of Bobby Henderson, can you? Vera likes him so much too."

"There *is* no point about him. He's just the usual sporting, stupid guardsman."

Felicity lit her husband's cigarette and left him.

Her dress this afternoon had been very carefully thought out to contrast with Vera's.

Vera was dressed in dull flame colour, becoming to her white skin and black hair. Felicity was in black and white. She wore a white hat, with a black velvet bow, and one enormous gardenia. It was impossible not to be pleased at Bertie's suppressed enthusiasm when she arrived. He was so fastidious about clothes, and she knew she was a real success to-day.

"Oh, Felicity, isn't it too *horrible*? The chief person can't come!" Vera was fluttering a telegram and evidently trying not to cry. "The *great* tenor, you know." She turned to Wilton. "Isn't it cruel at the last minute?"

"Oh, don't worry, darling. Most likely no one will notice it—you see you kept it dark as a surprise, luckily," said Felicity.

"And it *is* a surprise—to me!" said Vera.

"Oh, isn't the little harpy infant phenomenon coming?" asked Felicity.

"Oh yes, *that's* all right; he's here now, playing draughts with his mother in my room to prevent him getting nervous; and eating bread and jam. Thank goodness for that!"

"Oh, what sort of jam?" asked Wilton eagerly. "Pray don't keep it from me! Raspberry, greengage—*please* tell me, Mrs. Ogilvie!"

"Why, what *can* it matter?"

"It matters enormously."

"One would think you were a reporter," said Felicity.

"I'm not. I'm only a psychologist."

"Same thing," said Felicity.

"Well, anyhow, it's marmalade—so there!" said Vera.

"Oh, how delightful," exclaimed Wilton; "to match his hair, of course. Of course it's his mother's idea though. What a good mother she must be!"

"Oh, here he is, at last. Where are his wings?"

The boy, with his white suit and golden hair and small harp, looked, literally, angelic. There was a murmur of admiration.

"There oughtn't to be a dry eye in the room when he plays Schumann," said Felicity; "and fancy, Savile wouldn't come because he said he would long to kick him, and he was afraid Vera wouldn't like it."

"I rather agree with Vera there," said Bertie.

"No one would like, at one's musical party, to have one's artists kicked!"

"Everything is all right," said Felicity, as she smiled and bowed to some one.

"Why is everything all right? You gave one of your *special* smiles just now! Who was it?"

"De Valdez. It's rather jolly of him to have come here to-day. He was expected at the Spanish Embassy."

"Probably going on afterwards."

"Possibly not," said Felicity.

"I admit I admire De Valdez very much," said Wilton. "Caring for nothing on earth but music and philosophy, and the kindest-hearted man in the world, he has been literally hounded into society by admiring women, and all the fuss about him hasn't spoilt him a bit; he would keep a royal party waiting for luncheon while he ran down to Bedford Park to spend the day with an old friend."

"The point is," said Felicity calmly, "that he's a genius."

"Oh, is he? I don't know much about music," said Wilton rather jealously.

"I know you don't."

"The point is, that he's remarkably handsome," said Bertie.

"Now you're being disagreeable. Of course he's handsome, but that's *not* the point."

At this moment De Valdez joined them. Felicity took his arm and went down to tea.

The boy harpist created wildest enthusiasm; a little later De Valdez sang (after which nearly every husband present suggested it was time to go), and, on the whole, the afternoon was as great a success as these things ever are.

Quite late Bob Henderson arrived, full of tips—straight from the stable. Vera did not try to detain her lingering guests. Mr. Ogilvie never appeared on these occasions, but came home to dinner at eight, cross-questioned Vera, and did not listen to her answers in his usual amiable manner.

Jasmyn Vere was extremely anxious, as he always was, to have something a little out of the way for his party. He literally lived for society, and, in a minor degree, for Agatha. As he was a bachelor, and had devoted even more time and energy to knowing none of the wrong people than to knowing all the right ones, a party of his was looked upon as not a thing to miss, particularly as a decorous originality was always to be expected.

Lady Nora Wilton, a beauty of the early '80's, was a graceful and still pretty woman of forty-five; it was probably from her that Bertie had inherited his good looks and high spirits.

"What *can* we do just a little original?" Jasmyn had asked her.

"What sort of thing? You don't mean to be American and let all the people come dressed as children, or ask some wild animals to look in in the evening?"

Jasmyn threw up his hands in horror.

"My dear Lady Nora, don't make fun of me! No, some rather intelligent people are coming."

"Really? I thought your parties were always very smart!"

"There'll be some people who can talk, don't you know."

"What about?" said Lady Nora.

"Ah! that's the point! Now, I propose that when supper's on there shall be a special supper served at one table for ten in my little octagon room, and *with* the menu a subject for conversation with each item! It will, of course, not bore people, because, from the programme, they will see there is an ordinary supper-room too, and they can choose!"

"It will be a general conversation, remember; and people aren't very keen on that," said Lady Nora.

"Well, we shall see. So long as you don't disapprove (and one other lady to whom I shall speak of it). I think it's not a bad idea. I shall not have good music, Lady Nora. It isn't a concert—it's a conversazione."

"But you won't have *bad* music? I can't imagine anything bad in your house," said Lady Nora.

"No, but music that encourages talk. De Valdez once sang at my house— *Everybody* was there, and they *all* talked! He got up and said, in the middle of Although, that lovely song, 'Here are five hundred people who want to talk, and only one who wants to sing. The odds are not fair. I give in.' And nothing would induce him to go on. But as he remained and was most agreeable to every one, one could hardly call it the caprice of a spoilt artist. Indeed, I think he was quite right."

Lady Nora sighed. "But how uncomfortable! Well, then, you'd better have the Blue Hungarians and the Red ones too. Those who don't like the one can listen to the other."

He laughed and said, "Bertie's the image of his mother. I shall have a first-rate band and second-rate music."

"Agatha, Mrs. Wilkinson," was delighted at all the plans but said she simply *must* go to supper with Bobby Henderson, as it would be too marked to be escorted by the host.

As a matter of fact, nothing Agatha did was ever noticed, because she never did anything that was not extraordinary.

"Do I look all right, Chetwode?"

"Quite unnecessarily so," said Chetwode, and he gave her a look, which she recognised as the greatest compliment she ever received.

Her eyes brightened and she blushed.

"And who," said Chetwode, "may I ask, put it into your head to wear an entirely gold dress with your golden hair?"

She hesitated half a second.

"Oh! not the dressmaker? and it wasn't your own idea? I can only think of one other person. Do congratulate Wilton from me on his success as a designer."

"Chetwode! if I did ask him to design it, it was so that you should be pleased with the dress."

He smiled. "Quite so. And I am."

"Oh, won't you come and fetch me?"

"It's quite impossible. How late shall you stay?"

"I'll come back just when you like."

"Oh, enjoy yourself, dear. I'm going to stop at home."

He seemed to have regained the equanimity that for a moment he seemed to have lost.

Driving along, Felicity thought, "Perhaps if Chetwode *could* be a shade jealous of Bertie, it might be a good thing. Still, that sort of thing is so commonplace. *We* oughtn't to have to descend to it."

Surely Chetwode, who never went by the opinion of others, who absolutely judged for himself, and for whom general success by no means raised the value of his choice, could not care a shade more for his wife because she was admired by Wilton, and would care less for her if he did not think her incapable of admiring any one but himself.

"Are any of those eternal vulgar theories about love really ever true?" thought Felicity. Then wasn't Chetwode superior? Of course he was. That was why she loved him, and in wishing him to be an ordinary jealous man, she was wishing him to descend. However, when "Faute des roses" greeted her (exquisitely played by the Hungarians), and she was sitting in a bower of roses in her gold dress, with her respectfully worshipping and delightfully amusing Bertie, Felicity forgot her anxiety and thoroughly enjoyed herself. She was made much of, and admired; the homage was intoxicating, she was young, and she imprudently gave every one present the impression that she was flirting desperately with Bertie Wilton.

CHAPTER XIX

THE VELVET CASE

Savile, remembering that Chetwode had told him he was going away for 'a week end for ten days', and that Felicity had said he was going away for three days, went to see his sister. He had not received the promised wire from Chetwode, but instead a cordial invitation to lunch at the Savoy, in the course of which he told Savile that the whole thing had been laid before Teignmouth; that Teignmouth was slow but sure; that he was frightfully keen on arranging it, but said it can't be done in three days. Savile forbore to press the matter, and said that he, of course, disliked going back to school under the present circumstances; but if he could rely on Chetwode and Teignmouth he would only worry *two* more people. The spirit of emulation that Savile hoped to rouse in his brother-in-law was not observable. But Savile knew him to be a man of his word, and really felt certain of Teignmouth's influence—he had Aunt William and Jasmyn Vere up his sleeve. Aunt William was very rich and very interested in politics, being an ardent member of the Primrose League; Jasmyn Vere was so frightfully good-natured, and so anxious to set people at their ease, that if Savile appeared with a shy request (he smiled to himself as he thought of *his* being shy of old Jasmyn!) he would probably grant the request if he could. In fact, having seen in the *World* a paragraph speaking of Jasmyn as "one of the leaders of society, the brilliancy of whose entertainments was only equalled by their delightful originality" had decided Savile on the question.

"A chap," he said to himself, "who has a room arranged on purpose for bright conversation at supper, with the subjects on the menu, and spends thousands on orchids and gardenias for his parties, and admires Mrs. Wilkinson, and *yet* is at large, must have some peculiar power! I should have thought he'd got nothing in him; but he's got such a tremendous lot *on* him and around him, I suppose it does instead."

Thus Savile, lost in these thoughts, rang rather judicially at the house in Park Street that no ordinary house-agent could speak of without emotion as a noble mansion; others, more genuinely enthusiastic still, called it, with self-restraint, a commodious residence.

In the little blue-striped room that opened out of her bedroom he found Felicity in tears and a tea-gown. He remembered that day he had found Sylvia crying, and congratulated himself; first, that he was not a girl, secondly, that he and not another man had seen them thus grieving.

Felicity looked up and said, "Oh, Savile, you're just the person I want—an appalling thing has happened."

Savile sat down, lit a cigarette, and offered one to her, which she accepted.

Her manner was rather like that of a young man who, though he dislikes it, has decided to confide in a friend.

"Look here," she said, "I've had a wire from Chetwode to say he's going to stay on at the Tregellys till next week."

"Well, what of that? *That* can't be all, surely?"

"You're right, it's not. I was looking in one of his innumerable carved chests for some novels, when I found a locked velvet case." She stopped a minute. He was silent.

"I found a key that fitted it," she went on.

"Did you, though?" said Savile.

"In it I found a lovely porcelain picture of a woman. Blanche Tregelly was written on the back. Where he's staying, you know. I've never seen her. I vaguely knew Tregelly was more or less married: he was at Oxford with Chetwode; but as they live so far away I've never got to know them."

"Don't see your point," said Savile.

"*Why* has he got that picture, *and* is staying on?"

"Tregelly," said Savile, "probably gave it to Chetwode to get something done to it—get it framed or something."

"Chetwode's not a framemaker! Why is he staying on?"

"Because he's having a good time."

"You're shirking the whole thing. The point is that when he stays away so long, it isn't only racing."

"Of course not. At the Tregellys, it's bridge."

"Yes—and Mrs. Tregelly."

Angry tears again filled her eyes, but she brushed them away.

"You know Chetwode *does* admire beauty," she said.

Savile looked at the picture. "But only the very *most* beautiful. I've never yet seen him admire anything second-rate. Have you?"

She beamed and said, "Savile, *is* she second-rate?"

"Perhaps not, on porcelain."

"Savile, you *know* that if Chetwode likes her, she's not only pretty, but very charming. In fact, I'm certain Blanche is perfectly delightful! Pretending to oneself that one's rival is hideous and vulgar is a bit *too* cheap. It doesn't console me."

"You're worse than an ordinary woman, Felicity," said Savile, with a laugh. "What do you propose to do? Go and consult George Lewis?"

"You're worse than an ordinary boy. I'm consulting you."

"No, you're not. You're asking my opinion. Chetwode is very———" He paused. "I've never seen him look at any other woman."

"Let's face facts, dear," said Felicity. "It's not what we've seen, of course."

"What have you decided to do?" said Savile. "To write and tell him you've found the photograph?"

"Yes."

"I thought you wanted him to come home."

"Don't you?"

"Yes, rather!" said Savile. "And I don't think he *would* come home if he thought there was going to be a row of any kind. Lots of people love rows. He doesn't."

She looked rather at a loss, and then said, "Well, *what* would you do if you were in my place?"

He waited a minute and then said: "Don't you always write to him, when he's away, as if you were enjoying yourself?"

"Yes."

"Doesn't he ever think that there's a good deal of Wilton one—way or another?"

"I think he has," she said, brightening up a little.

"Well, for heaven's sake don't try that with Chetwode! The more he was riled, the more he'd say to himself, 'Of course she's enjoying herself. There's no harm in it. No hurry to go back.'"

"Chetwode," said Felicity, "is one of those very English men who would never own they're jealous unless things came to extremities, which, of course, naturally, they never would."

"Look here, you're making a fool of yourself," said Savile. "You're making yourself miserable over nothing at all." He stood up. "Don't do *anything* till after lunch, perhaps not till this evening. You've just had a bit of a shock. You'll find you're wrong. Telephone when you want me."

He kissed her and went away.

Felicity closed the velvet case. She then dressed very beautifully to go out, but when it came to putting on her hat she couldn't. It requires fairly good spirits to put on a modern hat and veil. She thought she would go downstairs and think. Then she saw Bertie's green motor at the door. She hesitated a moment about letting him come in; then she thought that she would tell him about it, and according to how he behaved, would test him once for all. If he didn't do exactly the right thing, she would never see him again.

As Wilton came in, all the fluent conversation and compliments, the gossip and jokes he had been saving up to tell her, died away on his lips. He saw she had been crying. He sat down further away than usual, and said—

"Don't tell me if you'd rather not. I'll go away, shall I? I'm quite sure you're not in the mood for me."

She said, "No, don't go."

There was a moment's silence.

"What was the party like last night at the Harpers?" she then asked.

"I haven't the slightest idea," he answered.

"But you must have been there? I didn't tell you I'd changed my mind about going. I meant to, and then at the last minute something rather dreadful happened, and I stayed at home."

"Yes, I'm almost sure I was there," said Wilton thoughtfully. "I think I must have gone if I expected to see you. But I don't remember anything about it. I must look in the *Morning Post* and see if I'm in the list of guests. I'm afraid you think I'm not the sort of friend to tell anything serious to, but really, Lady Chetwode, you're wrong there. If there was anything on earth that I could do——"

"It's something so annoying, so horrid," she said. Her voice was trembling.

"Tell me."

He looked so genuinely unhappy for her sake that, not being of the disposition that conceals its sorrows from the sympathetic, Felicity of course told him all about it.

He waited a minute, pale with interest, and then said—

"I appreciate your telling me this. But, of course, the whole trouble is entirely imaginary. Oh, I know that doesn't make it any better for the moment; but it's more evanescent."

"Imaginary? Why do you think that?"

"Well, the one thing that I pride myself on just the *least* little bit is an instinct—an instinct for temperament. I would undertake to swear that Chetwode is one of those exceptional people who only love one woman in their lives. He would never think of looking at any one except you. Of course, I know there are many men who don't really appreciate the most perfect woman if she happens to belong to them. But Chetwode isn't like that. He hasn't a fickle nature; he doesn't seek for variety and novelty. What you suppose is impossible to him. Not only now, but it always will be."

"You may be quite right about his temperament, Bertie. I dare say you are. But how do you account for the picture?"

"I don't. But there is an explanation. I don't pretend to be one of those wonderful thought-readers who, in some public calamity, see in the crystal everything they've read in the papers. You'll soon find out about it. It's some mistake."

She held out the picture to him.

"But she's very pretty, Bertie."

Wilton examined the picture.

"A very dull, harmless, insipid style of prettiness," he said consolingly. "The kind of face that once seen is never remembered, as has been so well said of the characteristic British face. This woman is devoted to her husband; goes to church every Sunday, takes great interest in parish work, adores her children——"

"How many has she?"

He looked at the picture again.

"From her expression, I should say two—two boys; and I'm quite sure she's very much more interested in their reports and their colds, their sins and their talents, than in—for instance—Chetwode, or in anything of the kind you seem to suggest."

"She never comes to London," said Felicity. "They live nearly all the year round at their country place."

"Of course she doesn't come to London. Why should she? She has a domestic face. Her home is her world. If she ever does come to town, she wears a short serge skirt and a blouse with tight sleeves—because she doesn't know they're coming in again—and takes one of the boys to the dentist."

"And you can see all that in the porcelain picture?" said Felicity, laughing.

"More. Far more. And all in your favour."

"But I think you're rather prejudiced, Bertie. You're such a convinced Londoner yourself that you think every one who lives in the country must be a paragon of virtue, just as people who live in the country suppose their London friends to be given up to wickedness and frivolity. Lots of people have a very good time in the country."

"No one knows that better than I do. I assure you I'm not a bit prejudiced. I quite believe and realise that people can have a good time anywhere. Why, even in provincial towns—what was that case at Bradford, that astonished everybody so much? However, my point is, that Mrs. Tregelly doesn't."

"Why? I think she looks very happy," said Felicity.

"Yes. Exactly. Happy, but perfectly calm. A woman placed as she is could not possibly look as calm as that if she had a secret purple romance with Chetwode, or with any other man. It just shows—if I may say so—how blind Love is. If this had happened to anybody else, you would be the first to see, on the face of it, that anything like a flirtation between the Lady of the Velvet Case and your husband is one of those hopeless impossibilities that only the wildly imaginative and charming people who have no relation to real life, like yourself, could possibly conceive."

Felicity seemed comforted.

"You think it utterly impossible?"

"Oh, I go further than that. I think it highly improbable. Can you see," continued Wilton, "this gentle, harmless creature, a woman capable of having her portrait painted on porcelain, from a photograph, and framed in crimson velvet, who never in her life had a secret except when she concealed from her husband her real reason for sending the housemaid away in order to give the girl another chance by giving her a good character—can you see *her*, I say, privately slipping this enormous case into Chetwode's small and reluctant white hand just as she was going to church, and saying, 'Keep it for my sake'?"

"You make the whole thing so ridiculous, Bertie, I begin to think you're right, but still it's very extraordinary that he did have it."

"Our not knowing the reason is not nearly so extraordinary as your explanation."

"But I can't wait for the real explanation. Suspense is torture," she said.

"But delightful—or there'd be no gambling in the world. Still, if you dislike it, why not telegraph?" Wilton suggested.

"Because, you see, if there's nothing in it, I should appear so utterly absurd. And if there was, *is* it likely that Chetwode would wire and say so?"

"Scarcely. You have sparks of real genius, Lady Chetwode, I must say! I never thought of that! The best way would be to make him come back as quickly as possible. Of course, he'd return if you were ill?"

"Rather. Besides, I am. Very."

"So you are. Then write to that effect."

"I think I will, but not yet." She remembered Savile's advice to wait till after dinner.

"May I ask," inquired Wilton, "if you're delaying in order to confide in women? This, I know, seems very impertinent of me, but I can't help advising you not. You'd be so sorry afterwards! When you go and tell Vera that it is all right after all, however pleased she is, there'll always be an uncomfortable feeling on your side that perhaps she doesn't quite believe you—that she thinks you're making the best of it. And Miss Sylvia will be so gloriously indignant and jealous for you that she won't do you any good."

"I know, Bertie. You are absolutely right. But I never do confide in women—only in men whom I can trust. Like you—and Savile."

"Thank you. And how right you are! Then if you're going to delay any action in the matter and put the picture aside, what are you going to do to-day?"

"I half promised Vera to meet her marvellous new palmist, Madame Zero, at her house this afternoon."

She took Vera's note out of a long grey envelope sealed with an Egyptian seal.

"It seems she's *too* wonderful. Only one or two people are going."

"Mrs. Ogilvie kindly asked me," said Bertie modestly. "Of course you'll go and hear what the soothsayer has to say about the velvet case?"

"Perhaps, but I'm not sure.... I feel restless.... I must say, it does seem unlikely there could be much harm in a woman who has her portrait painted in porcelain from a photograph—by the young lady at the photographer's, I dare say, who makes the appointments and touches up the negatives. And yet—perhaps that very innocence—that sweet, blank expression—even the tight sleeves and the two boys may make her all the more attractive!"

Wilton got up.

"Good-bye," he said. "You're perverse. It's no use, I see, telling you not to worry; but please try to realise there's no occasion."

"Wouldn't you say just the same if you thought there had been occasion?" she persisted.

"Absolutely. But that doesn't prove I'm not sincere now."

He pressed her hand with a look that he hoped conveyed the highest respect, the tenderest sympathy, a deep, though carefully suppressed passion, and a longing to administer some refined and courteous consolation, and went away.

Wilton was only twenty-five, so, naturally, as soon as he got home, he tried the expression in the mirror, and was horribly disappointed in it.

"I must have looked as if I'd suddenly got an awful twinge of neuralgia," he said to himself.

"It shows how careful one ought to be. Confound it!"

Felicity, however, was not troubling herself about Wilton or his expressive looks. The complicated glance, which he feared was a failure, had not even been seen by her. What he had said cheered her for the moment, and *au fond*, at the back of her brain, with her real sound common sense, she did not actually believe in the cause of her grief. But passion and jealousy, unfortunately, are not governed by sound common sense; they work in circles. Argument and reasoning have but a temporary effect on them; they come back to the point at which they started.

As she looked at Mrs. Tregelly's picture, the feverish chills of suspicion again took possession of her. She told herself repeatedly that she had only been married a year, that Chetwode was in love with her, and had always seemed cold to other women. But he was continually away. He was charming and attractive. Perhaps the other women he met thought *she* lived for amusement and was utterly neglectful of him. She was afraid she had been imprudent in being seen so much with Wilton, but Chetwode never seemed, really, to mind. He trusted her as she deserved, and as she ought to trust him. Considering the terms that they were on—far more like lovers than husband and wife—it would be real treachery on his part. He was incapable of treachery. She would trust him.

Then the image of Chetwode making love to that pretty woman abruptly forced itself on her mental vision in spite of all reasoning, like a sudden violent physical pain, and she burst into tears.

She controlled them as soon as possible, for she strongly dissented from the old-fashioned idea that a good cry was consoling. On the contrary, she thought that the headache and unbecoming traces of emotion that followed tears had a particularly depressing effect, and left one with nerves. She resolved to dismiss the subject for the moment, anyhow, and to go to Vera's in the afternoon to meet Madame Zero and two or three of Vera's most favoured and intimate friends.

CHAPTER XX

ZERO, THE SOOTHSAYER

Mrs. Ogilvie looked more Egyptian than ever to-day. She always dressed for her parts; and as a believer in the Unseen, she felt it right, in honour of the sibyl, to wear her hair very low, with some green pins in it, long earrings, and a flowing gown, with Japanese sleeves.

"Vera, you're almost in fancy dress," said Felicity, as she arrived. "It's very becoming; but why?"

"Am I, dear? Well, it's as a sort of compliment to this wonderful girl. I've been draping the little boudoir with gold embroideries—and burning joss-sticks, too (though they give me a headache). I thought it would bring out her gift—make her feel more at home, you know."

"Good gracious, is she an Algerian or an Indian or anything?"

"Oh dear no, darling. Of course not. She's a Highlander, that's all. It runs in her family. To know things that haven't happened, I mean."

"But that *will* happen?"

"I hope so, I'm sure. She's in there," said Vera, pointing to a beaded curtain, that concealed the small drawing-room. "She's gazing into the crystal for Bob Henderson. You shall go next, darling."

"I should have imagined Captain Henderson the very last person in the world to dabble in the occult, as they call it in the newspapers. I should have thought he would laugh at superstition."

"Oh, so he does, dear, but he wants to know what's going to win the Derby."

"From all I've heard about racing," said Felicity, "if he wants to know that, he'd better wait till it's run."

"Oh, Felicity, don't cast a sort of damper on the thing before him! Perhaps he'll be converted. He may take it quite seriously now. It would do him good, he's so matter-of-fact."

At this moment a very loud and hearty laugh was heard, and Captain Henderson appeared through the beaded curtain and joined them.

"What a long time you've been," said Vera.

"She's a pretty girl," said Captain Henderson.

"Any success?" asked Felicity.

"She saw some horses in the crystal. But as she didn't know their names, it was no earthly use to me. Says I'll back the winner for a place, though. She's got second-rate sight—second sight, I mean."

"A great many of these old Highland families have," said Felicity seriously, to please Vera.

"Have they, though? She says she's half Irish," said Henderson, with his characteristic puzzled look. "She's been telling my character too—reading between the lines, you know, the lines on my hand. She doesn't seem to think much of me, Mrs. Ogilvie." He laughed again.

"As soon as she's had some tea," said Vera, ringing, "you must go in, Felicity. We mustn't tire her. It's frightfully exhausting work."

"Must be," assented Bob.

"It takes it out of her ever so much more with some people than with others," said Vera.

"Ah, it would," said Bob solemnly, shaking his head.

"I suppose complicated people are more wearing than the simpler kind," said Felicity. "There's more in them to find out."

"You mean it must have been pretty plain sailing with me?" said Henderson.

Here Wilton arrived.

"There's something about the tone of your delightful home to-day," he said as he greeted Vera, "that makes me feel curiously Oriental. I don't exactly know what it is, but I feel I want to sit down cross-legged on a mat and smoke a hookah. How do you account for it?"

"You 'hear the East a-calling,' and all that sort of thing," said Henderson, laughing. "Eh?"

"Yes. But perhaps after all it's only the east wind. No, it's the incense some one's been burning. At your shrine, of course, Mrs. Ogilvie. What a talent you have for creating the right atmosphere."

Vera was highly flattered.

"And now I think you might go in, Felicity," she said.

Felicity found a young girl with bright pleasant eyes, seated in front of a little yellow table. She had a magnifying-glass on one side of her and a crystal ball on the other. She was very neatly dressed in the tailor-made style, and had no superfluous decorations of any kind. Anything less like a sibyl could not be easily imagined.

Felicity took off her glove and placed her hand on a yellow cushion. As she did so, she remembered charming things that Chetwode had said about her hands, how he had compared them to white flowers; and she sighed....

"You're vurry sensitive indeed," said the palmist, with a slight American accent. "Your nerves seem to me to be vibrating."

"But isn't that usual?" said Felicity shyly. "I thought nerves always did."

"Just hold the crystal in your hand for a minute or two. Thank you. Ah! there's a slight cloud on your horizon at this moment, but it will pass away—I see it passing away."

"What else do you see?"

"I see you in a large space surrounded by a hurrying crowd. There are bookstalls, trucks of luggage, trains, I can't say precisely what it is."

"Surely a railway station?" said Felicity.

"You are perfectly right. I should fancy from this that you are either going to take a journey by rail, or that you are going to see a friend off."

"Do you advise me to take the journey?"

"I fear advice one way or the other would have vurry little effect. I am a believer in Fate. Either you're going to take that journey, or you're not, in spite of anything I may suggest to the contrary."

And the palmist smiled archly, then leant back and closed her eyes. Felicity wondered if she were tired with the noise of the railway station. But she opened them suddenly, and took Felicity's hand, which she looked at through the magnifying-glass.

"This is a most interesting hand. Mrs. Ogilvie's gentleman friend, who was in here just now, also had a vurry interesting hand. She's a lovely woman, and her hand is most interesting too...."

She paused.

"You have a curious temperament. You are easily impressed by the personality of other people. You are impulsive and emotional, and yet you have a remarkable amount of calm judgment, so that you can analyse, and watch your own feelings and those of the other persons as well as if it were a matter of indifference to you. Your strong affections never blind you to the faults and weaknesses of their object, and those faults do not make you care for them less, but in some cases attach you even more strongly. You are fond of gaiety; your moods vary easily, because you vibrate to music, bright surroundings, and sympathy. But you have depth, and in an emergency I should say you could be capable even of heroism. You have an astonishing amount of intuition."

"What a horrid little creature!" said Felicity.

"Your tact and knowledge of how to deal with people are so natural to you that you are scarcely conscious of them. You should have been the wife of a great diplomatist."

"But aren't they always very ugly?" asked Felicity.

"You're not as trivial as you wish to appear," replied the palmist; "you are very frank and straightforward, but reserved on subjects that are nearest your heart.... Is there any question you would like to ask me?"

"I should like to know," said Felicity, giving herself away as the most sceptical victim always does, "whether the person I care for is true to me."

As she said the words she thought they sounded as if she were a sentimental shop-girl whose young man had shown signs of ceasing his attentions. And why not? She felt exactly like that shop-girl. It was precisely the same thing.

The palmist smiled sympathetically, and said, "He has no other thought but you. Believe me, you are his one object, and he will be true to you through life."

"And how on earth can you see that?" said Felicity, unreasonably cheered, though inclined to laugh.

"I can't say. It's not possible to explain these things; but here, you see, your Fate line is a wonderfully good one, and it goes parallel (if I may say so) with the heart line. Now, if the *Life* line had crossed it, or reached the Mount of Luna—well, I should have said you were destined to disappointment in love. But that is not so. You have a lucky hand. You have artistic tastes, but would never work in any direction, except the social—that is why I say a diplomatic circle would have suited you."

Felicity feared the soothsayer was getting rather bored with her, so she said—

"Thank you. Have you any advice to give me before I go?"

"Yes. It would be to your advantage if you used your head less and followed your natural impulses more."

"Then I must throw something at Chetwode's head when I see him," thought Felicity.

As she got up, "I see two beautiful children in your hand," added the palmist.

"Oh, when?" said Felicity, starting, and accidentally knocking down the crystal ball.

"Within the next few years," answered the palmist cautiously.

"Now it's my turn," said Bertie, as Felicity joined them. "Do tell me," he said in an undertone, "was there anything about me in your hand?"

"Rather not—not a trace of you. Why, what did you expect?"

"Oh, then I don't think much of her. I thought at least she would see my initials all over your lifeline. I assure you, any good palmist would. I'm afraid she's a fraud."

"I trust not. She was rather consoling," said Felicity thoughtfully.

"She was wonderful with me," said Vera, as Bertie disappeared. "I wonder what her nationality really is."

"Thought you said she was a Highlander." Bob looked more puzzled than ever.

"Well, so she is, partly. In a way. Unless I'm mixing her up with some one else."

"And yet Zero isn't a Scotch name," remarked Felicity thoughtfully.

"No; and it's a rotten name too—doesn't suit her a bit. But it's not her real name. On her card is Miss Cora G. Donovan," said Bob.

"How do you know?" asked Vera sharply.

"Well, I had to ask her address. I've got to see her again, don't you know. Before the Derby. To make sure. Only fair to give it a chance," said Bob, rather apologetically.

"She's an Irish American," decided Felicity.

"Is she? I dare say she is. I wonder what she'll say to Wilton now," said Bob meditatively.

"Bertie will tell her everything he knows about himself, and about every one else in whom either he or she takes the slightest interest. Then he'll go on to tell her character, and prophesy her future, and she'll confide in him, and he'll give her good advice. He always tells fortune-tellers their fortune. That's why he's so popular in the occult world," said Felicity.

"Wonder they stand it," said Bob.

"Why, naturally, they enjoy it. Mustn't they get frightfully bored, poor things, with talking all the time about other people, and be only too thankful and delighted to be allowed to talk about themselves a little? Fancy how refreshing it must be; what a relief! Think of the tedium of always bothering about perfect strangers—pretending to care about their luck and their love affairs, their fortunes and their failures, and all their silly little private affairs. It must be absolutely fascinating for them to meet a person so interested in other people as Bertie."

"Perhaps he only does it out of kindness," said Vera. "I shouldn't wonder. Asks them questions and shows interest just to please them."

"Well, I call it infernal cheek," said Bob resentfully.

"Not at all. Some people aren't always absorbed in themselves," said Vera, with a reproachful look as she gave Bob a cup of tea.

At this moment Sylvia was announced. She looked very happy and excited.

"I hope I'm not too late. I only want to ask Madame Zero *one* question. I shan't be a moment."

"Of course you shall, dear, and I know you won't keep her long, as she'll be very tired now after seeing us all. Now, Sylvia"—Vera turned to Felicity—"is unusual. She's neither curious about other people nor intensely interested in herself."

"I don't mind how interested people are in themselves, so long as they're interesting people," said Felicity.

"Do you call it taking too much interest in oneself to want to back a winner just once—for a change? I had tips straight from the stable about three horses yesterday, at Haydock Park. And I give you my word, Lady Chetwode, they all went down."

"Dead certainties never seem to do anything else," Felicity answered.

"Mind you, it was partly my own fault," continued Bob. "If I'd had the sense to back Little Lady for the Warrington Handicap Hurdle Race—as any chap in his senses would have done after her out-jumping the favourite and securing a lead at the final obstacle in the Stayer Steeplechase, I should have got home on the day—or at any rate on the week. But then, you see, I'd seen her twice refuse at the water—and I was a bit too cautious, I suppose!"

"You generally are," murmured Vera, but he did not hear, having sunk into a racing reverie.

Bertie appeared through the curtains.

"I congratulate you, Mrs. Ogilvie. Your soothsayer is a marvel."

"Isn't she!" triumphantly said his hostess.

"It's the most extraordinary thing I ever came across in my life. She simply took my breath away. Yes, tea, please. She's a genius."

"Does she seem very exhausted? Or do you think Sylvia might just ask her one question?"

"Oh, surely—Miss Sylvia's so reposeful," said Bertie. "I fancy I could answer the one question myself," he added in a low voice to Sylvia, as he held the curtains back for her to pass.

"She's been a success with you, I see," said Felicity.

"She has, indeed! She got right there every time—as she would say herself in her quaint Eastern phraseology. She has one of the most remarkable personalities I ever met. No one would believe what that girl has gone through in her life—and she's been so brave and plucky through it all! Did you notice what remarkable hands she has?"

"I told you so," laughed Felicity. "She's been confiding in Bertie and he's told *her* fortune! I knew it."

Bertie coloured slightly as he ate a pink cake.

"Shouldn't have thought that of her," grumbled Bob. "She seemed a sensible sort of girl."

"My dear Henderson, don't be absurd. After her wonderful divination about me, of course I couldn't help asking her a few questions as to how she developed the gift—and so on—and she told me the most amazing things."

"She would, I'm sure," said Vera sympathetically. "I wonder if she'll tell Sylvia anything about what Mr. Ridokanaki is doing."

"Oh, I can tell you all about him," said Bertie readily. "He's having a very good time in Paris just now. I hear he's always about with the Beaugardes. Miss Beaugarde's a very pretty girl just out of her convent. Her mother's working it for all she's worth. Clever woman. I shouldn't be surprised if it came off, if Madame Beaugarde can make him believe the girl's in love with him for himself."

"You see we really need no sibyls and soothsayers when we have Bertie," said Felicity. "To know him really is a liberal education. He knows everything."

"Sort of walking *Harmsworth's Self-educator*," said Bob rather bitterly, as he took his hat.

Sylvia returned, evidently content. She told Felicity afterwards that Madame Zero had seen her in the crystal in a large building of a sacred character, dressed all in white and holding a bouquet. The sound of the chanting of sweet boys' voices was in the air. What could it possibly mean?

Whether or not Madame Zero had demonstrated her gifts so convincingly as to have converted a sceptic, there was no doubt that she had perceptibly raised the spirits of the whole party (not excluding her own), so the séance was quite deservedly pronounced an immense success.

CHAPTER XXI

"THE OTHER GIRL"

Savile had received a note from Dolly, asking him to go and see her in the square. Savile was feeling rather sore because Dolly and her French friends had gone to a fancy ball the night before, a kind of semi-juvenile party where all the children wore powdered hair. Dolly had offered to get him an invitation, but he scornfully refused, knowing she was going to dance the cotillon with Robert de Saules.

So depressed had he seemed that evening that Sylvia had played "Home, Sweet Home" to him five or six times. It made him miserable, which he thoroughly enjoyed, and he was feeling altogether rather cynical and bitter when he got Dolly's little note. He had heard nothing more of Chetwode, and intended to see Jasmyn Vere before he left; there was only another week before the end of his holidays. Should he be cool to Dolly? or not let her know how he felt about the fancy ball?

As soon as he arrived he thought she looked different. The powder had been imperfectly brushed out of her hair; also she had been crying. She greeted him very gently. She wore a pretty white dress and a pale blue sash.

"I suppose you've been very happy these holidays?" said Dolly.

"Oh, I don't know! I've had a great deal to—to see to," said Savile.

"I suppose you see a great deal of The Other Girl?" said Dolly.

Considering that he had only been once to Wales to hear his idol sing at a concert, there was a certain satisfaction in giving Dolly to understand that he hadn't really had half a bad time; so he smiled and didn't answer.

"Is she grown up?" asked Dolly.

Savile was cautiously reserved on the subject, but seemed to think he might go so far as to say she *was* grown up.

"Did you have fun last night?" he then asked.

"No. I was simply miserable."

"Why?"

"I kept the cotillon for Robert, though he hadn't exactly asked for it, and when the time came the girl of the house, who is eighteen, actually danced it with him!"

"Hope you didn't show you cared."

"No, I didn't; but I danced with a lot of stupid little boys, and I was so bored! Besides, I *hate* Robert. Wasn't it mean of him? He went to supper with this grown-up girl, who was awfully amused at his foreign accent, and he behaved as if *I* was just a child, a friend of his little sister Thérèse. Now, do you think, Savile, as a man of the world, that I ought ever to speak to him again?"

"When's he going away?" asked Savile.

"Next week; at the end of the holidays."

"If you cut him dead as he deserves," said Savile, "it's treating him as if he mattered. Of course, you *really* showed you were offended?"

"Well—I suppose I did. You see, his head was quite turned by these old grown-up girls making a fuss about him."

"What a rotter!" said Savile kindly. "Well, do you still like him?"

"No; I simply hate him, I tell you," said Dolly.

"Then don't bother about him any more."

Savile forbore to say, "I told you so!" He was however naturally gratified.

"What I should like," said Dolly candidly, "would be to be able to tell Thérèse—who would tell Robert—that I'm engaged to *you*!"

"Well, tell her so, if you like."

"Oh, what a brick you are! It's not very truthful though, is it?"

Savile said that didn't matter with foreigners.

"It is a pity," Dolly murmured, with a sigh, "that it can't *be* true!"

"Yes—isn't it?" said Savile.

"After all," said Dolly, "you're not exactly *engaged* to the other girl."

"How do *you* know?"

"Oh, I'm sure you're not."

"As a matter of fact I'm not."

"But you think she might marry you when you're grown up?"

Savile smiled. "Before there'll be a chance of marrying her, I shall be dead of old age."

"When shall you see her again?"

"Next Wednesday, the day before I go away."

Felicity had promised to take him to a concert where he might not only see her but possibly even be introduced to her in the artists' room, through the good nature of De Valdez, who had been told of Savile's romantic devotion.

But Savile was now feeling rather tenderly towards Dolly, who had evidently learnt by experience to put her trust in Englishmen. In fact, at this moment he was thoroughly enjoying himself again.

"I don't think after all I *shall* say I'm engaged to you," said Dolly sadly. "There's something depressing about it when it isn't true."

"Oh well, let's make it true."

"Really; but what about The Other Girl?"

"You don't quite understand. That's a different thing. There she is—but—that's all. It's nothing to do with being engaged to you."

She looked bewildered.

"But is she very fond of you?"

"Not at all," said Savile.

"Oh, she *must* be," said Dolly admiringly.

Savile blushed and said, "My dear girl, she doesn't know me from Adam! So there!"

"Then why on earth did you break it off before?" said Dolly, clapping her hands and beaming.

"Well, you see, I think a good deal of her," said Savile, "and then, what with one thing and another—you didn't seem to want me much."

"But I do *now*!" said Dolly frankly.

"Oh, all right. Well, look here, old girl, we'll be engaged, just as we were before; but—I must have my freedom."

"Indeed you shan't," said Dolly, with flashing eyes. "I never heard such nonsense! What do you mean by your freedom? Then can't I have mine too?"

"Rather not! What a baby you are, Dolly. Don't you know, there's one law for a man and another for a woman?"

She gasped with rage.

"I never heard such nonsense in my life. I shall certainly not allow anything of the kind. Either we're engaged or we're not."

"Very well, my dear, keep calm about it. It doesn't matter. Here I offer," said Savile, "to please you, to be engaged again, and you don't like my terms. Then it's off."

"I think you're more cruel than Robert," said Dolly.

"But not such an ass," said Savile.

"And not so treacherous," admitted Dolly, who seemed as if she did not want him to go.

"Just tell me what you *mean* by your freedom," she said pleadingly.

"As I'm placed," said Savile mysteriously, "all I want is to see The Other Girl once, on Wednesday. I shall probably only have a few words with her. Then I believe they are going away, and I'm going back to school."

"*They* are going away," said Dolly, mystified. "Then is there more than one?"

"More than one? Good God, no! One's enough!" said Savile, with a sigh.

"After all," said Dolly very prettily, "I do trust you, Savile."

Savile was intensely pleased, but he only answered gruffly, "That's as well to know!"

"Then I'll try not to be jealous of her. I won't think about her at all."

"No, I shouldn't," said Savile.

"Then we are engaged," said Dolly again, "definitely?"

"Of course we are. And look here, you've got to do what I tell you."

"What am I to do?"

"You're to be jolly, just as you used to be; you're to come and meet me here every day, and—I'm not quite sure we really saw Madame Tussaud's properly that day."

"Well, you were so cross, Savile."

"I shan't be cross now. I'll take you there, and we'll have tea. Could you go to-day?"

"I think, just to-day," said Dolly, "I *might* be allowed. A particular friend of mamma's is coming to-day whom she hasn't seen for ages. She told me not to come into the drawing-room."

"All right. Run in now and fix it up."

"Mamma," said Dolly, "will expect me to go to the De Saules; but as my holiday task is about Charles II, and we shall see him at the waxworks——"

"I leave all that to you," said Savile.

"Very well, then. Come and fetch me at three. I'm sure I can arrange it. Won't Robert be surprised!"

"One more thing," said Savile rather sternly. "Remember that I don't care *two* straws whether he's surprised or not, and I don't want his name mentioned again."

"Then it's not to annoy him?"

"No. It's to please me. Us."

"Very well."

She gave him her hand.

"And you won't even—now that we're engaged properly—give up seeing—The Other Girl on Wednesday?" she pleaded.

Savile frowned darkly.

"You may be sure I shall do the right thing," he said rather grandly, "and you're not to refer to her again. I've told you I shall only see her once, and that's enough for you."

"I think you are very tyrannical," said Dolly, pouting.

"That won't do you any harm, my dear."

"And—you don't seem fond of me a bit!"

"Yes I am. What a fool you are! I'm awfully fond of you, Dolly."

"And are you very happy?"

"Yes, very fairly happy," said Savile. "And mind you have that powder all brushed out of your hair. I don't like it."

They walked to the gate.

"I really have missed you awfully, dear," said Savile gently.

"You have your faults, Savile, but you are reliable, I *will* say that."

"Rather," said Savile. "I'll bring you a ring this afternoon or to-morrow."

"What! How lovely! But I shan't be allowed to wear it."

"Then keep it till you can."

"It's very sweet of you. Good-bye, Savile."

"Good-bye, dear. I say, Dolly?"

"Yes?"

"Oh, nothing!"

CHAPTER XXII

SAVILE AND JASMYN

Savile had written asking Jasmyn Vere to see him on a matter of importance.

Jasmyn promptly and courteously made an appointment, and spent the intervening hours chuckling to himself at the solemn tone of the letter, and wondering what in Heaven's name the child could possibly want.

He received Savile in a kind of winter garden, or conservatory at the back of his house, and went to meet him with the most charming cordiality, to put the boy at his ease. He would have been rather surprised had he known that something about his reddish hair, and his mouth open with hospitable welcome against the green background, reminded the boy irresistibly of an amiable gold-fish.

"So delighted, dear boy, that you should have thought of me. Anything, of course, in the world that I could do for you, or for any of your charming family, I should look upon as a real privilege. Have a cigarette? You smoke, of course? You oughtn't to. Take this nice comfortable chair—not that one, it's horrid—and tell me all about it."

"Thanks, awfully," said Savile seriously, intensely amused at his host's nervous, elaborate politeness, and trying hard to repress the inclination to laugh that Jasmyn always inspired in him. How fluttered and flattered the dear old thing seemed! Savile wasn't a bit frightened of him.

"I knew you know all about things, Mr. Vere," said Savile, accepting a cigarette and a cushioned deck-chair, "and I thought I'd ask your advice about something."

Jasmyn was completely at a loss. Could it be a question of a tenner? It so often was. But no, he felt sure that it was nothing quite so commonplace, or quite so simple.

In a few minutes he had heard and thoroughly taken in the whole story.

He was most interested, and particularly sympathetic about Sylvia, though from his own point of view—the worldly social-conventional view—she ought to have done better. As he thought it over he walked up and down the winter garden.

Some birds were twittering in gold cages among the palms and plants, and every now and then he stopped to talk to them in the little language one uses to pets, which irritated Savile to the verge of madness.

"I know of one thing," said Jasmyn, "and only one, that might do. I know a charming young fellow who's been ordered to travel for a year, and needs a companion. He doesn't want to go, a bit; but his relatives might be able to persuade him to, if he took a fancy to Woodville, and I'm sure he would. He's just a little mad. That would be delightful for your friend if he could get it: yachting for six months; a motoring tour in Italy; all sorts of nice things. He's a man called Newman Ferguson."

"But you see, it's Woodville himself who wants a companion," said Savile. "I don't think in his present state he'd be particularly keen on being shut up alone on a yacht with a raving lunatic, and struggling with him in a padded state-room. I shouldn't think he'd do for the post. Then, I don't see how his going away for a year would help."

"True, my dear boy. How clever you are! Well, I suppose I must think it over, and look round."

Savile looked very disappointed.

"I mustn't let you go without giving you some hope, though. I see how much your heart is in it!" said Jasmyn good-naturedly.

"Can you give any general sort of advice?" Savile asked. "How *does* a chap get things?"

"It's very, very difficult, dear Savile, and it's getting more and more difficult—unless you're related to somebody—or have heaps of money. The really best thing, of course, for our friend, would be to go into some kind of business. I'll look out and see if something turns up. Now look here," and Jasmyn put his arm in Savile's, "if it's something of that sort, and it's merely some—a—cash for capital that's required, let him look upon me as his banker. Tell him that, Savile. You'll know how."

"No, I shan't know how, Mr. Vere. He wouldn't like it. And then, besides, you see he doesn't know anything about it—I mean about my coming to you like this. Sylvia doesn't, either. Of course, old Woodville would be very pleased if I went and told him he'd got some capital appointment. He'd soon forgive me then for my cheek in interfering. But not what you've just said. Awfully jolly of you, though."

Jasmyn took a few steps back and stared at Savile.

"You mean to say you've undertaken this all on your own? Why, you're a marvel! Haven't you really mentioned it to a soul?"

"As a matter of fact," said Savile scrupulously, "I *did* just mention something about it—not your name or theirs, of course—to the girl I'm engaged to. But she doesn't know any more about it than she did before."

Jasmyn exploded with laughter.

"Savile, you'll go far. So much prudence combined with so much pluck—why you'll end by being Prime Minister!"

"I shouldn't care for that. Besides, I can't," Savile said apologetically, "I'm going into the army."

"And what about *your* engagement?"

"Nothing about it. It won't make any difference."

"To whom?"

"Why, to me—or to *her* either—so far as that goes."

"Tell me why you're so keen about Woodville, and what you're taking all this trouble for, old boy?"

"Why, for my sister, of course!" Savile answered, surprised.

"You're a dear good boy. And you shan't be disappointed. As soon as I hear of anything I'll let you know, and we'll talk it over again. When do you go back to school?"

"In a few days," said Savile, getting up to go.

"Poor chap! Well, well, we'll see what happens. Must you go now? Cheer up. It's sure to come all right. And I say, Savile——"

"Yes?"

"Remember me kindly to your fiancée, won't you?"

"Of *course* I shan't! She's never heard of you. Her mother doesn't let her read the papers, not even the *Morning Post*. And besides, it's quite a private engagement."

"You can trust me, Savile. Just tell me one thing," Jasmyn said, with an inquisitive leer. "Is she dark or fair?"

"Not very," said Savile.

CHAPTER XXIII

SAVILE AND BERTIE

As Wilton was convinced that a satisfactory ending to the trouble was imminent, he naturally felt a great desire to be, somehow, the cause of Felicity's renewed happiness; to get, as it were, the credit of it. That his admiration (to put it mildly) should take the form of chivalrous devotion would be, at least, something; especially as it was evident that no other satisfaction was likely to come his way. Her one other confidant was Savile; and it struck Bertie that a kind of confederation with the boy might be a success.

Besides, it would be fun.... Savile hadn't ever been cordial with him, but had retained a rather cool, ironical manner, as if suspicious of his attitude. Bertie had that peculiar vanity that consists in an acute desire to be able to please everybody. He had always felt absurdly annoyed at being unable to gain Savile's approval. And the wish to make a conquest of every one connected with Her was no doubt part of his reason for sending Savile an urgent message to come and see him immediately.

He was now waiting in his rooms at Half-Moon Street for the boy's arrival.

Savile had promised to come round in a reserved and cautious note, but the request had given him intense gratification and joy. He felt he really was becoming a person of importance.

The instant Savile arrived he made up his mind that as soon as he was grown up and able to have rooms of his own, they should be arranged, in every particular, exactly like Wilton's. But instead of the Romney, the one picture that Bertie possessed, and which bore so striking a likeness to Felicity, he decided he would have in its place a large portrait of Madame Patti.

"Look here, old boy, perhaps you think this rather cheek of me. But we both know that your sister's rather worried just now."

"She *is* a bit off colour," admitted Savile.

"Well, why on earth don't you put it straight?"

Savile's expression remained impassible. He said:

"Think I ought?"

"You're the only person who can."

"All right," said Savile. "I'll write to Chetwode."

"It'll take some time, writing and getting an answer," said Wilton.

"No good expecting an answer," said Savile. "He's the sort of chap who never writes letters unless they're unnecessary."

"And Lady Chetwode will be in a hurry," observed Bertie.

"You know her pretty well," said Savile.

"Then what's your idea?"

"I shall send him an enormous wire," said Savile—"he's more likely to read it than a letter—explaining the whole thing, and telling him to come home at once. I shan't ask for an answer."

"Why not?"

"Because I shouldn't get it."

"Good. That's a capital idea. But—a—Savile, can you afford these luxuries? I couldn't have, when I was a boy at Eton.—Look here, let me——"

Savile turned round and looked Wilton straight in the face.

"No, thanks," he said deliberately, shaking his head. Bertie's colour rose.

"But, my dear boy, why on earth not?"

"Oh, I expect you know," said Savile. Then feeling a little remorseful for the rebuff, he added: "Don't you bother about that. Besides, Aunt William gave me a couple of quid the other day to buy a ring for the girl I'm engaged to. I shan't buy it just yet. That's all."

Bertie concealed his amusement.

"Then you'll have to keep the poor girl waiting," he said.

"Keep her waiting?" said Savile. "Of course I shall. It's a very good plan." He got up and took his hat. "Makes them more keen. Don't you find it so?"

"In *my* unfortunate experience nothing makes them keen at all, unless, of course, it's some one one doesn't want. And then everything does."

"Hard luck!" said Savile, shaking his head wisely, and took his leave, thinking with a smile that Wilton, having obviously got the chuck, was trying to keep in favour by playing the good friend. "He's not half a bad chap," thought Savile. "And I'll send that wire; it's a good idea."

He stood under a lamp at the corner of Half-Moon Street and counted his money.

"Confound it, I've only got a bob! It'll just pay for a cab to Aunt William's."

Thoroughly enjoying this exciting and adventurous life of diplomacy, he arrived at his aunt's. She was dressing for dinner. Nevertheless, for Savile, she came downstairs in a magenta wrapper.

"I hope there's nothing wrong, my dear boy," she said.

"No, everything's quite all right. But—you know what you gave me the other day, Aunt William?"

"Yes, dear."

"Sorry to say it's all gone."

"Oh, Savile!"

"Before I go back," said Savile, with a note of pathos in his voice, "I've one or two little presents I'm awfully keen on giving. I dare say you understand."

She didn't understand, but she gave him a five-pound note.

He beamed, and said, "Well, of all the bricks!"

"You promise me to spend it wisely, Savile dear. But I know I can trust you."

"Rather! This will be more frightfully useful than you can possibly imagine. Well, it seems beastly to rush in and get all I can, and then fly; but I've simply got to go. Besides, you want to dress," said Savile, looking at the wrapper.

"Yes. Get along with you, and I do hope that you won't turn out a dreadful, extravagant, fast young man when you're grown up," said Aunt William, with relish at the idea.

Savile smiled.

"Don't you worry about *that*, Aunt William! Why, you're thinking of ages ago, or Ouida, or something. There's no such thing nowadays as a fast young man, as you call it. They're always talking about how ill they are, or how hard up, and how they don't want to be bothered with women."

"How do you mean, dear?"

"Why, they're frightened to death of girls marrying them against their will—or getting mixed up in things—oh, I don't know! Anyhow, women seem to think it a great score to get hold of one. So that proves it, don't you think?"

"Then why is it that your sisters, for instance, are always surrounded by admirers?" said Aunt William.

"First of all, surrounded is bosh. Just as much as what you're always saying, that Sylvia has the world at her feet. They happen to be particularly pretty, and Felicity's jolly clever. But after all, they have only one or two each—admirers, I mean. And *they*—the girls—are exceptions."

Aunt William sighed.

"You're very worldly-wise, and you're a very clever boy, but you don't know everything."

CHAPTER XXIV

THE EXPLANATION

The fact that Chetwode was returning more than a week sooner than she had expected, seemed to Felicity a hopeful sign. She hesitated for about half an hour as to whether or not she should go and meet him at the station. Doubt and dignity suggested remaining at home, but impatience carried the day.

As she was waiting on the platform, the prophecy of Madame Zero occurred to her, and she thought to herself, with a smile—

"She doesn't seem so bad at prophesying what one's *going* to do. It's when she prophesies what one *ought* to have done that the poor dear gets out of her depth."

When he had arrived, and they were driving off together, she thought he looked neither more nor less serene and casual than usual; his actual presence seemed to radiate calm and dispose of anxiety; her suspicions began to melt away.

They had dined together, and talked on generalities, and neither had mentioned the subject. Chetwode's intense dislike to any disturbing topic infected Felicity; she now felt a desire to let him off even an explanation. She wished she had never seen the velvet case, or, at any rate, that she had never mentioned it to any one. He didn't, she fancied, look as if he were deceiving her in any way. His affection was not more marked than usual, nor less so. She observed there was no tinge in his manner of an attempt to make up for anything. Yet the question had to be asked.

"What did you do most of the time there?" began Felicity.

"Nothing. Played bridge."

"By the way," said Felicity, "you've never told me what *Mrs.* Tregelly's like."

"Of course I haven't. She isn't like anything."

"Isn't she very pretty?"

"Oh, I suppose she's all right—for Tregelly," said Chetwode.

"Then if you don't admire her at all, would you mind telling me why you have her portrait locked up in a velvet case?" demanded Felicity in a soft, sweet voice.

"I wonder!" said Chetwode.

"Oh, don't be so irritating. Don't you *know* you have it?"

"I haven't known it long."

His coolness roused her, and she said angrily—

"Then you ought to have known. I've been fearing that your casual ways are a very convenient screen for——"

"For what?" he asked, smiling. He was disposed to tease her for having doubted him.

She did not answer. He came and sat next to her.

"And so you would have cared?"

"Cared? I should think so. I've been miserable!"

"What a shame! I'm very sorry—I mean, very glad. But you might have spared yourself all this worry, dear, if you'd thought two minutes."

"How? How do you prove that what I imagined isn't true?"

"My dear girl, could you seriously suspect me of wanting to possess a coloured portrait on porcelain taken from a photograph? Did you think I'd have such a thing in the house—except inadvertently?"

"It's a pretty face," she said.

"But it's an appalling picture! Don't I *care* about things? I hope I haven't got any silly vanity about it, but I don't think I ever have anything wrong—I mean, artistically."

He looked round the room with the uncontrollable pride of the collector.

"No, my dear," he went on, "you've done me an injustice. From you I'm really surprised."

"But *anything*, as a souvenir of a person you like very much ..." she said hesitatingly.

"Oh, all right!" he answered. "Do you suppose if I'd an awful oleograph of *you*, even—that I'd keep it as a souvenir? Good heavens, Felicity, one doesn't bring sentiment into *that* sort of thing! You ought to have known me better."

She waited a moment.

"Then on those grounds alone I'm to consider I'm utterly wrong?"

"Rather! Suppose you'd found a wonderful early sketch by Whistler or Burne-Jones, say, of a pretty woman—even then I should never have believed you'd be such a Philistine as to suppose that the person who *sat* for it had any interest for me. But a thing like that!" He laughed and shrugged his shoulders.

"How did it get there?"

"How did it get there?" he answered. "Last time I stayed with them, Tregelly sent it up to me for my critical opinion on it as a work of art." He laughed. "It made me so sick that I locked it up, and dropped or lost the key, or else I told the man to put it away. As he's an ass, I suppose he packed it among my things. I suppose Tregelly thought I gave it to his wife, and she thought I gave it back to him, as I heard no more about the thing then. But this time, as soon as I arrived," he smiled, "it was passionately reclaimed by both—and I promised to have a look."

Felicity clapped her hands.

"Then I'll send it back at once, and—will you have a look?"

"Good God, no! Never let me see the thing again." He took up a paper as if tired of the subject.

"Did you come back to look for it?" she asked.

"I came back because I received a three-volume novel wire from Savile, explaining what he called the situation."

"Fancy! Isn't he wonderful?"

"He's the limit," said Chetwode, laughing.

"But you might tell me, dear Chetwode; it isn't really for her that you go there?"

"Really, Felicity! I hardly ever see her! She's always busy with her children or rattling her house-keeping keys. Oh, she's all *right*—suits Tregelly, poor chap! Are we through now?" he asked, with patience.

"No. Won't you kiss me and forgive me?"

"Presently," he said, turning a page of the paper.

"May I just say that nothing of this sort could ever have happened if—if you didn't go away just a *little* too much? From the very first you know you were always absolutely free. I've the greatest horror of bothering you, or tyrannising in any way, but don't you think it's gone a little too far? If we hadn't been rather separated, I couldn't have made such a mistake about you. Suppose you'd found, privately locked up, a similar portrait of Bertie Wilton, say, wouldn't *you* have thought things?"

"Wilton's an ass," said Chetwode. "But he does *know*. To give him his due, I couldn't have found a similar portrait of him. He isn't capable of allowing such a thing to exist."

"Well, say a good portrait," said Felicity. "Do let us be perfectly frank with each other."

"We will," said Chetwode. "I *am* rather sick of Wilton."

"He's really an awfully good boy," said Felicity.

"Then let him be a good boy somewhere else. I'm tired of him."

"I'll see less of him," she answered.

"Good!" said Chetwode.

"And—I know it was a very long speech I made just now, but don't you think I'm right?"

"I didn't hear," he answered. "I was listening to your voice."

"Then must I say it all over again? I *really* want you to take it in, Chetwode," she said pleadingly.

"Say it all over again, and as much more as you like, dear."

"And then will you tell me you haven't heard?"

He threw down the newspaper.

"Very likely. I shall have been looking at your lips."

CHAPTER XXV

THE QUARREL

"The other day," said Sylvia, "you were perfectly sweet to me. I was really happy; I knew you loved me, and that was quite enough. Now again I feel that miserable doubtfulness."

"May I ask," said Woodville, who was sitting in front of a pile of papers, while Sylvia was leaning her head on her hand opposite him at the table, "how it is that you're here again?"

He spoke in a tone that was carefully not affectionate and that he tried not to make irritable.

"Certainly. I arranged to go out with Felicity—before papa—and then I telephoned to her that I had a headache."

"Isn't that what you did on Thursday?"

"No; on Thursday I said I was going to the dentist. And came in here instead."

"Do you intend to do this often?" he asked.

"Yes, continually."

He rustled the papers.

"Why shouldn't I? Don't you like it?" she said.

"I can't help thinking it's rather risky. Suppose Felicity comes and finds you in blooming health?"

"Surely I can recover from my headache if I like? Besides, she telephoned to me to get some aspirin. She won't expect me to be down till this afternoon, and she won't come till then."

"*Did* you get some?"

"Frank, what idiotic questions you ask!"

There was a pause.

"Don't you think, dear," she said, "this is very jolly, to arrange to have two hours like this alone together?"

"Oh, delightful! But I don't see what's the good of it, as we're placed."

"Not to have a nice quiet talk?"

"I have nothing to talk about." He seemed nervous.

"Are you going to be like this when we're married?" asked Sylvia in a disappointed voice.

"Not at all!"

"Oh, I'm *so* glad! If you'll excuse my saying so, Frank darling, you seem to me to have a rather sulky disposition."

He seized the papers and threw them on the floor.

"Sulky? *I, sulky?* You never made a greater mistake. You're not a good judge of character, Sylvia. Don't go in for it. Leave it alone. You'll never make anything of it, you haven't the gift. As it happens, I have a very good temper, except that now and then I'm 'rather violent when roused,' as the palmists say, but sulky—never!"

Sylvia seemed to have made up her mind to be irritating. She laughed a good deal. (She looked most lovely when laughing.)

"What are you laughing at?" he asked.

"At you. Pretending to be violent, good-tempered. Of course you're neither. What you think is self-control is merely sulkiness."

His eyes flashed.

"What do you want?" he said, in an undertone.

"Why, I want you to be sensible and jolly; like you were that day at Richmond."

"How can I be like I was that day at Richmond? It was a lovely day; we were in the country; it was our escapade. It was an exceptional case."

"Oh dear! Then will you only be *like that* as an exceptional case?"

"My dear child, you don't understand. When a man has—has work to do," he said rather hesitatingly.

She laughed again.

"Work! It must be frightfully important work if you throw it on the floor from temper."

He bore this well, and answered, picking up the papers, "Important or not, it's what I'm here for—it's what your father pays me for. How on earth he can think I'm the slightest use to him I can't imagine."

"Oh, he knows you're not, really, dear," said Sylvia soothingly. "But he's grown used to you, and to have a secretary makes him feel he's a sort of important public man. Don't you see?"

"What! I'm *not* useful to him?" Woodville asked angrily. "I should like to know——" Here he stopped.

"I suppose you think he won't know what to do without you when we're married," said Sylvia.

"Oh, I do wish you'd leave off saying that, Sylvia."

"Saying what?"

"When we're married. You have no idea how irritating you are, darling."

"Irritating? Oh dear, Frank, I'm so sorry. Do forgive me. Perhaps it is rather bad taste, but I say it to cheer you up, to remind you you have something to look forward to. Do you see?"

She looked at him sweetly, but he would not meet her eyes.

"Perhaps you're *not* looking forward to it?" she said in a piqued voice.

"Sylvia, would you mind going away?"

"Oh, all right. Very well. I won't disturb you any more. It's very sweet and conscientious of you to bother about the papers. I'll go. Shan't you want me always with you when we're married?"

"Never!" he answered. "At least, not if I have any other occupation."

Her eyes brightened.

"Oh! then it isn't that I worry you, but I sort of distract your attention. Is that it?"

He made no answer.

"I'm afraid," said Sylvia sadly, "that we shall quarrel dreadfully."

"Quarrel? Rot!" said Woodville. "We shall *never* quarrel. You'll do exactly what I tell you—and I shall devote myself to doing everything for your good."

"If I thought you meant anything as dull as that I should break it off at once," said Sylvia. "The programme doesn't sound attractive."

He laughed. "How do you think it ought to be then?"

"There'll be only one will between us," said Sylvia, "that is to say, you'll do everything I want always, Frank. Do you hear? Won't you answer? Well, I see you're in a bad temper." She got up. "Good-bye." She held out her hand. "I shall hardly see you again all day, and Frank——I see you don't want to kiss me once before I go."

"Oh, you see that, do you?"

"Of course, I think you're an ideal man and a darling in every way, and I love you very much, but I think it's a pity you're so cold and heartless." She came nearer to him.

"Don't say that again," he said, with a rather dangerous look.

"But you are! You're absolutely cold. I think you only love me as a duty."

At this Woodville seemed to lose his head. He seized her in his arms and kissed her roughly and at random, holding her close to him.

"Oh don't, Frank. How can you be so horrid? You're making my hair untidy. Oh, Frank!"

When he at last released her, he walked to the window and looked out. She went to the looking-glass with tears in her eyes, and arranged her hair.

"I didn't think," she said reproachfully, "that you could behave like that, Frank!"

He made no reply.

As she stood at the door she said, pouting, "You didn't seem to care whether *I* liked it or not."

"And I didn't!" said Woodville. "I wasn't thinking about what you'd like."

"And—shan't you ever think about what I'd like?"

"Oh, I shall think a great deal about what you'd like," said Woodville, "and I shall see that you like it. But that will be different. I don't apologise; you brought it on yourself."

"I'll try to forgive you," said Sylvia. "But now, I really *have* a headache."

"Take some aspirin," said Woodville.

"How peculiar you are! Then I'm not to come in to-morrow morning?"

"Do as you like; you know what to expect."

"Why, you don't mean to say you would behave like that *again*?"

"I shall make it a rule," he answered.

"It's unkind of you to say that, because now you know I *can't* come."

"This sort of thing is becoming impossible," said Woodville. "You make it worse for me."

"I'm sorry," she said gently. "I assure you it wasn't what I wanted, really."

"I dare say not. But you don't understand."

"Will you promise never to break the compact again?" said Sylvia, looking up at him sweetly.

"Will you go?" he answered in a low voice.

This time she went.

CHAPTER XXVI

VERA'S ADVENTURE

Mrs. Ogilvie stopped at Hatchards' and fluttered in her usual vague way to the bookshop.

"I want some serious books," she said. "Something about Life or Philosophy or anything of that kind."

The young man said he understood exactly what she meant, and produced a new book by Hichens.

"But that's a novel! I want a real philosophical work."

"*Maxims of Love*, by Stendhal," suggested the young man.

"What a pretty book! No—I mean something *really* dull. Have you anything by Schopenhauer? or Dr. Reich?"

The young man said that he thought anything of that kind could be got, and meanwhile suggested Benson.

"No, that's too frivolous," said Vera seriously. She then bought casually *Mr. Punch on the Continong*, and left orders for books by Plato, Herbert Spencer, and various other thoughtful writers, to be sent to her without loss of time.

She then drove to the dressmaker's. Whenever she had fallen freshly in love she got new dresses and new books. To-day she ordered a rather ugly but very expensive new evening dress, rather weakly, at the last moment, buying a tea-gown that she did not want.

Then she began to think she wanted to see Felicity, and yet she liked to feel she had a sort of secret to herself for a little while. It really had been a declaration, and Felicity had a way of inquiring into these things and examining them until they were entirely analysed away.

No, she thought she would like to see him again before saying anything about it. He was a serious man. She had met him at a musical German lunch, where she had not expected to be amused. He looked as if he had suffered—or, perhaps, sat up too late.... He had dark blue eyes, which she chose to call violet. He talked, beautifully about philosophy. He made her feel she had a Soul—which was just the sort of thing she needed; and though he was at a musical German lunch, he was neither musical nor German, and his satisfaction in sitting next to her instead of next a celebrated German singer who was present was both obvious and complimentary. Yet what had he really said?

He had said, "My dear Mrs. Ogilvie, human nature is human nature all the world over, and there's no getting away from it, try how you will. Oh! don't get me on my hobby, because I'm afraid I shall bore you, but I'm a bit of a philosopher in my way."

How clever! But what did he mean? He told her to read philosophy. He said she had the eyes of a mystic. She had spent several minutes looking in the mirror trying to see the strange mysticism he saw in her eyes, and remembering the prophesies of Zero.

They talked a long time after lunch in the deep window seat, where the music was audible but not disturbing, and she had not asked him to call. She was always asking people to call, and they always called, and it was always the same, nothing ever came of it. Probably some instinct told her she would see him again, or she could not have resisted. Finally he said, "We have known each other in a previous existence. This is an old friendship. I shall come and see you to-morrow."

"Not to-morrow—Thursday," said Vera, thinking she would not have time to get a new dress. So he was coming to-morrow. Perhaps he would give her some new philosophy of life. He would make the riddle of existence clear. He had bright and beautiful eyes, but—and here came in Vera's weakness— she could not make up her mind even to fall in love without some comment of Felicity's.

Supposing Felicity said it was charming and just the right thing for her, how delightful that would be! On the other hand, she might make one of those terrible enlightening little remarks that smashed up all illusions and practically spoilt the fun. How right she had been about Bobby! "*Not worth worrying about.*" How right about many other people! Then Felicity now settled nothing (with regard to people) without consulting Bertie. Instead of taking a person just as he appeared as Vera did, "Charming man, most cultured— I'm sure you'll like him," as the hostess, Mrs. Dorfenstein, had said, Bertie would know everything about him—who his father and mother were, why he happened to be at the German lunch, his profession, his favourite hobbies, what was his usual method, and a hundred other things likely to prevent any sort of surprises. Really, Felicity and Bertie together were a rather formidable couple of psychologists. Felicity often amused herself by experimenting on the people that Bertie had discovered. What Vera feared more than anything else was that Mr. Newman Ferguson would be pronounced a very simple case. When she came home from her drive she saw a letter—a new handwriting, which she instinctively felt certain was from Mr. Ferguson. Therefore, although she was alone, she put it in her muff, went and locked herself into her room, and began to read it.

The first thing that struck her was the remarkably beautiful, carefully formed handwriting, and the immense length of the letter.

Pink with joy and excitement, her hat and furs still on, she read—

"*My dear Mrs. Ogilvie, ... Ships that pass in the night.... Friends signalling.... Elective affinities.*" ... "Oh, good gracious!" She glanced hastily at the signature. "*Strange as it may seem, I am now and for all time your devoted slave, Newman Ferguson.*"

At last Vera's wish had been granted; some one had really fallen in love with her. But she had not patience to read the letter through. Her friend's counsel was necessary instantly.

She flew to the telephone. "Felicity!—Oh, there you are!... I meant not to tell you, but something *so* exciting has happened.... Yesterday at the German lunch ... a wonderful person.... His name?—Newman Ferguson.... Have you ever heard of him?... You'll find out all about him from Bertie.... Thanks.... Couldn't I see you to-day? Very well, then, ring me up if you have any news.... Keep calm indeed! I *am* keeping calm!"

Mr. Ogilvie's knock was heard. Vera hid the letter and went downstairs.

Felicity walked in at ten o'clock the next morning. Vera thought she had rather a peculiar expression.

"Don't you think it sounds lovely?" said Vera.

"I should like to see the letter."

They read the letter together.

"What an extraordinary conglomeration! I can't make head or tail of it."

"He's coming to see me this afternoon."

"Is he, though?"

"What do you know about him?"

"Well, Bertie knows the Dorfensteins who gave the lunch, and he says they don't know anything about him at all. He was just sort of brought instead of some one else."

"Does Bertie know him?" asked Vera.

"Well, yes, he does a little, and he says he's very nice generally."

"What *do* you mean by 'generally'?"

At this moment the servant came in and said, "Mr. Newman Ferguson has called and wishes to see you immediately."

"Good heavens!" said Vera.

"Show him in!" said Felicity.

They were sitting in the little yellow boudoir, Mr. Ogilvie having just gone out.

Mr. Newman Ferguson came in, carrying an enormous bouquet. He bowed most courteously, offered Vera the bouquet, and said—

"Human nature is human nature all the world over, my dear lady. There's no getting away from it, try how you will."

"It's very early for you to think of such a clever thing to say," said Felicity.

"I trust you don't think it's too early to call."

"Not at all," said Vera, looking terrified.

"The only thing is," said Felicity, "that my friend and I are just going out."

She stood up.

"Then pray excuse me," said Mr. Newman Ferguson; "I will call a little later on to-day instead."

"Where did you say you were staying now?" said Felicity.

"I'm at the Savoy at present, but I hope to move very soon," he said, with a meaning look.

Felicity saw him to the door where he had left his cab, came back, and stood silently looking at her friend and the bouquet.

"My dear Felicity, there's no doubt he's madly in love with me," said Vera. "Can you deny it?"

"My dear Vera, he's raving mad," answered Felicity.

"What?" cried Vera.

"Is it possible that you don't see it?"

"But look at that clever letter!" said Vera.

"It's the maddest letter I ever read. Besides, dear, I know about it. Don't distress yourself. Bertie says he was always eccentric, but sometimes he's quite all right for years. Then, any sudden excitement, especially Falling in Love——"

"Then you own he *did* fall in love with me?"

"Oh, of course, of course! Certainly! No one denies that. But I really think we ought to write to the Dorfensteins and get them to tell the Savoy people to look after him. It's very sad. He has rather a nice manner—nice eyes."

Vera buried her face in her handkerchief.

"Now don't worry, darling," said Felicity affectionately. "Be out when he calls, and I'm quite sure we shall soon find some one quite sane who will amuse you just as much."

"Never!" sobbed Vera. "It's just like my luck! Oh, and the books I ordered, and the new dress. I can never bear to look at them."

"It's a very good thing we found it out," said Felicity.

"But how on earth does Bertie know?"

"He knows everything—about people, I mean—and he's always right. In fact, he sent you a message to ask you to be very careful, and said he'd come and see you about it."

"Rather cool! It seems I can't have *any* secret to myself now," panted Mrs. Ogilvie.

"Well, you see, dear, you *did* ask me to get all the information I could, and after all I only told Bertie you *met* Mr. Ferguson. He guessed that he would fall in love with you, and bring you a bouquet early in the morning, and write you a lot of letters about philosophy."

"How did he know?"

"Well, if you don't mind my saying so, dear, it's because it's what he always does."

Vera began to laugh.

"Tell Bertie he need not trouble to call about it, I'd rather forget it."

"Oh, of course he won't *now*!"

"He doesn't know, then, that I was in love with him? Besides, I wasn't."

"Certainly he doesn't. Besides, you weren't."

"I hate the sight of that bouquet," said Vera.

"Yes, let's send it away; and now come for a drive with me."

"All right, dear. I say, couldn't we countermand those philosophical books?"

"Yes, of course we will. What do you feel you'd like instead?"

"Oh, something by Pett Ridge," said Vera, recklessly.

CHAPTER XXVII

AUNT WILLIAM'S DAY

It was a chilly spring afternoon and Aunt William was seated by the fire doing wool-work, for she disapproved of the idle habits of the present day and thought that a lady should always have her fingers employed in some way; not, of course, either with cards or cigarettes. She was getting on steadily with the foot-stool she was making; a neat design of a fox's head with a background of green leaves. In the course of her life Aunt William had done many, many miles of wool-work. It was neither embroidery nor tapestry; it was made on canvas with what is known for some mysterious reason as Berlin wool; and was so simple that it used to be called the Idiot Stitch; but the curious elaboration of the design and sort of dignified middle-Victorian futility about it cast a glamour over the whole, and dispelled any association of idiocy from the complete work. A banner screen was now in front of the fire, which Aunt William had worked during a winter at St. Leonards, and which represented enormous squashed roses like purple cauliflowers, with a red-brown background—a shade called, in her youth, Bismarck brown, and for which she always retained a certain weakness.

It was her day, and on Aunt William's day she invariably wore a shot-silk dress, shot with green and violet; the bodice trimmed with bugles, the skirt plain and flowing. Aunt William did not have that straight-fronted look that is such a consolation to our modern women who are getting on in years, but went in decidedly at the waist, her figure being like a neat pincushion. Her voice was deep, her mind of a somewhat manly and decided order, so that the touches of feminine timidity or sentiment taught her in early youth sat oddly enough on her now. In reality she hated wool-work, but did it partly from tradition and partly from a contrary disposition; because other people didn't like it, and even because she didn't like it herself.

Her first visitor was a very old and dear friend of hers whom she particularly disliked and disapproved of, Lady Virginia Harper. Lady Virginia was a very tall, thin, faded blonde, still full of shadowy vitality, who wore a flaxen transformation so obviously artificial that not the most censorious person by the utmost stretch of malice could assume it was meant to deceive the public. With equal candour she wore a magnificent set of teeth, and a touch of rouge on each cheek-bone. To Aunt William's extreme annoyance Lady Virginia was dressed to-day in a strange medley of the artistic style combined oddly with a rather wild attempt at Parisian smartness. That is to say, in her cloak and furs she looked almost like an outside coloured plate on the cover of *Paris Fashions*; while when she threw it open one could see that she wore a limp *crêpe de chine* Empire gown of an undecided mauve, with a waist under the arms and puffed sleeves. On her head was a very smart bright blue flower toque, put on entirely wrong, with a loose blue veil hanging at the back. Had anything been required to decide the question of her looking grotesque, I should mention that she wore long mauve *suède* gloves. That settled it. A gold bag dangled from her left wrist, and she carried a little fan of carved ivory. She looked, naturally,—or unnaturally—slightly absurd, but had great distinction and no sort of affectation, while an expression that alternated between amiable enthusiasm and absent-minded depression characterised her shadowy indefinite features.

Aunt William received her with self-control, and she immediately asked for tea.

"Certainly. It is half-past three, and I regard five as tea-time. But as you wish, dear Virginia." Aunt William pulled the bell with manly vigour and ill-tempered hospitality.

"Have you heard that *divine* new infant harpist? He's perfectly exquisite—a genius. But *the* person I've come to talk to you about, Mary, is the new singer, Delestin. He's perfectly heavenly! And so good-looking! I've taken him up—quite—and I want you to be kind about him, dear Mary."

"I'll take two tickets for his concert," said Aunt William harshly. "But I won't go to the concert and I won't come and hear him sing."

"Now that's so like you, Mary! He isn't *giving* a concert, and I *want* you to hear him sing. He's too charming. Such a gentle soft creature, and so highly-strung. The other day after he had sung at my house—it was something of Richard Strauss's, certainly a very enervating song, I must own that—he simply fainted at the piano, and had to be taken away. So, if you give a party, do have him, dear Mary! You will, won't you?"

"Most certainly not! A protégé of yours who faints at the piano wouldn't be at all suitable for one of *my* Evenings, thank you, Virginia."

Lady Virginia did not answer. She evidently had not heard. She never listened and never thought of one subject for more than two seconds at a time. She used a long-handled lorgnette, but usually dropped it before it had reached her eye.

"Oh! and there's something else I wanted to speak to you about. A sweet girl, a friend of mine (poor thing!), has lost her parents. They were generals or clergymen or something, and she's obliged to do something, so she's going in for hats. So sensible and brave of her! She's taken the *sweetest* little shop just out of Bond Street. Do, dear, go and get some toques there, for my sake. Won't you?"

"*Some toques?*" repeated Aunt William. "I don't know what you mean. Hats are not things you order by the half-dozen. I have my winter's bonnet, my spring bonnet which I have got already, a sun-hat for travelling in the summer, and so forth."

"I got a beautiful picture-hat from her," said Lady Virginia dreamily. "An enormous black one, with Nattier blue roses in front and white feathers at the back—— only five guineas. But then she makes special prices for me, of course."

"No doubt she does," said Aunt William.

"Of course I can't wear it, my dear," continued Virginia. "I hate to attract attention so, and I look too showy in a picture-hat with my fair hair. But it was a kindness to the girl. Poor girl!"

Aunt William was boiling over.

"Of course you can't wear it. Do you imagine you can wear the hat you've got on now, Virginia?"

"What this? It's only a little flower toque."

"At *our* age," said Aunt William, "*only* little flower toques, as you call them, should be left to younger people. Oh how much nicer you would look, Virginia, in a black or brown silk dress, and a close bonnet with strings, say with a chrysanthemum or two, and a few bugles if you like. It would be so much more suitable."

"What *is* a close bonnet?" asked Lady Virginia, trying to concentrate her thoughts and not in the least offended.

The arrival of Savile at this moment created a diversion. His air of inscrutability and self-restraint was neither more nor less marked than usual; but, to the acute observer, it would have been evident that he was crammed with suppressed and exciting information.

"You remember my nephew, Virginia? My brother James's only son, you know." Aunt William spoke proudly, as if his being an only son were some remarkable merit of his own.

"Not at all," murmured Savile indistinctly.

"Oh, is he really? What a darling! I adore children," said Lady Virginia, benevolently smiling at him. "And *so* tall for his age, too!"

"You don't know his age," snapped Aunt William.

"No, I don't; but I can see he's tall—a very fine child. What do you learn at school, darling?"

"Oh, nothing much," said Savile, with patience.

Lady Virginia laughed inconsequently.

"What a clever boy he is! Children *are* so wonderful nowadays! When Delestin was only six he played all Chopin's Valses and Liszt's Rhapsodies by heart. Of course that's some time ago now, but it shows what boys *can* do."

"By Jove!" said Savile.

"Who's your great friend at school, dear?"

"Oh—I suppose Sweeny's my *greatest* pal. He's in the eleven," added Savile explanatorily.

"Oh, yes! I daresay—a very nice boy too. He has a marvellous likeness to you, Mary dear," Lady Virginia said, using the long-handled glass, "especially about the—well—the ears—and forehead. Are you musical, my dear?"

"I like some of it," said Savile, with a sigh.

"You're like James, too," said Lady Virginia, "and I think I see a look of his mother, Mary."

"You never saw her, and you know it," said Aunt William, who always tried in vain to pin Virginia down to facts.

"Yes, but that was merely by chance," said Lady Virginia, getting into her cloak. "Then I shall expect you, Mary, to come and hear Delestin play? Oh, no, I forgot—you said you couldn't. I'm so sorry; but I *must* fly.... I've a thousand things to do. You know my busy life! I'm the President of the Young Girls' Typewriting Society, and I have to go and see about it. How we poor women ever get through the season with all the work we do is more than I can ever understand."

Aunt William became much more cordial at the prospect of her friend's departure, and when Virginia had at last fluttered out, after dropping the gold bag and the ivory fan twice, Savile said—

"Do you expect *many* more visitors like that to-day, Aunt William?"

"None like that."

"Well, while you're alone I've got some news to tell you. Sylvia would have come herself, but she's engaged—this afternoon."

"Not engaged to be married, I suppose!" said Aunt William, with a sort of triumphal archness.

"Yes, you've hit it in once. At least, up to a certain point. It'll be all right. But the Governor's a bit nasty—and the fact is, we want you to come and see him, and sort of talk him over, you know."

"Savile! Do you mean it? How charming!... But who's the young man—and what's the objection?"

Savile thought a moment, and remembered her tinge of snobbishness. "He's Sir Bryce Woodville's nephew. Chap who died. I mean, the uncle died. It's Woodville, *you* know!"

"Your father's secretary?"

"Yes, and a rattling good chap, too. Sylvia's liked him for ages, and he didn't like to come up to the scratch because he was hard up. Now something's turned up. Old Ridokanaki's written him a letter—wants him to go into his bank. He'll have three thousand a year. It's only *habit* with the Governor to pretend to mind. But a few words with you will settle it. I'll tell you more about it later on."

"I *am* amazed at the news, Savile. He's a very fine young man, but——"

"He's all right, Aunt William."

"But I thought the Greek gentleman with the unpronounceable name was madly in love with Sylvia himself? I've often talked it over with your father. He and I took opposite views."

"So he was, but he's got some one else now. It's simply *got* to come off. Now *will* you come and see us?"

"Certainly. When?"

"As soon as possible. I wish you'd come now."

"But this is my Day, Savile! How can I go out on my *Day*?"

"Of course you can. You'll have heaps of other days, but none like this—for Sylvia."

Aunt William hesitated, then her intense romantic curiosity got the upper hand.

"Savile, I'll come back with you now! Do you think James will listen to reason? He never agrees with me. And I don't know yet what to think myself."

"Of course he will. You're a brick, Aunt William. I'll tell you more about it in the cab. It's as right as rain for Sylvia, or you may be pretty certain *I* shouldn't have allowed it," said Savile.

To get Aunt William to go out on her Day, a thing she had not done for thirty years, was so great a triumph that he had little fear of not getting her to be on the right side. He knew she always made a point of disagreeing with his father on every subject under heaven, so he rubbed in Sir James's opposition, and gradually worked on her sentimental side until she was almost tearfully enthusiastic.

"How shall I behave? Go right in and tell your father he must consent?—or what?"

"Play for safety," said Savile.

CHAPTER XXVIII

THE TWELFTH HOUR

Sir James was extremely annoyed with the weather. In his young days, as he remarked with bitterness, spring was spring, and it didn't thunder and snow in April. He was prattling pompously of the sunshine in the past, when a sudden heavy shower of hail, falling rather defiantly in spite of his hints, made him lose his temper. Sir James, looking angrily up at the sky, declared that unless it stopped within half an hour he would write to the *Times* about it.

Whether or not this threat had any real meteorological influence, there is no doubt that the clouds dispersed rather hastily, the sun hurriedly appeared, and the weather promptly prepared to enable Sir James to venture out, which he did with a gracious wave of the hand to the entire horizon, as though willing to say no more about it.

Sylvia had been as anxious for the thermometer to go up as her father himself, for it was several days now since she had seen Woodville alone. And he had been nervously counting the minutes until the moment of freedom, having, to-day, a stronger reason than ever before to desire a quiet talk.

Woodville had expressed some remorse—not much, though considerably more than he felt—for what Sylvia called his conduct during their last interview, and she meant this morning to forgive him.

"I've only come," said Sylvia, sitting opposite him at the writing-table, "because I saw you were *really* sorry for ... the other day. *Are* you sorry?"

"Awfully."

"*That's* not very flattering," said Sylvia.

"I wanted you, too, dreadfully this morning," he said eagerly. "I've got something wonderful to tell you—to show you."

"Anything dreadful?" she asked, turning pale.

He took out a letter.

"Listen! Since the other day I had made up my mind to go away from here. I began to see I couldn't bear it. At least, for a time."

"What!" cried Sylvia, rising to her feet.

"Yes. But you needn't worry. I've changed my mind, darling. And before I tell you any more——"

He leant across the writing-table and kissed her softly, and at some length.

"Now," he said, "read this letter."

"From the Greek fiend! Is he trying to take you away from me again?"

"No, he's not. Read it aloud."

Sylvia read:—

"RITZ HOTEL, PARIS.

"'My dear Woodville,—In the short time since I had the pleasure of seeing you, certain changes have come over my views on many subjects; my future is likely to be entirely different from what I had supposed, and I felt impelled to let you know, before any one else, of the unexpected happiness that is about to dawn for me.'

"Oh, Frank, how long-winded and flowery!"

"Never mind that. It's his style always when he's sentimental. Do go on reading."

Sylvia went on. "'I was greatly disappointed at first to know you were unwilling to go to Athens. Perhaps, however, it is better as it is. Briefly, I have found in la *ville lumière* what I had longed for and despaired of—a reciprocal affection—that of a young and innocent girl—'"

"Sylvia, don't waste time. Go on!"

"'My heart'"—Sylvia continued to read—"'is filled with joy; but I will not take up all my letter to you with ecstatic rhapsodies; nor will I indulge myself by referring to her beauty, her charm, her Madonna-like face and sylph-like form. Her extraordinary affection for me (I speak with all humility)—tempered as it naturally was by the modesty of her age (she is barely seventeen)—was, I think, what first drew me towards her. We are to be married in May. You know that the sorrow of my life was that I had never been loved for myself. I have been called a successful man, but in my own heart I know that this is the only real success I have ever had during fifty-five years. It is certainly a great pleasure to think, as I do, that I shall be able to give my Gabrielle all (humanly speaking) that she can desire....'"

"Will you stop laughing? You *must* get through the preliminaries, Sylvia!"

"It seems all preliminaries," murmured Sylvia.

"'But, in my happiness, your troubles are not forgotten: and I hope now to be able to remove them in all essentials.

"'First, let me ask you to remember me to Miss Sylvia, and to tell her that with the deepest respect I now formally relinquish all hopes of her hand.'

"Very kind of him! He seems to claim some merit for not wanting to marry us both," Sylvia cried.

"'No doubt you remember my telling you of a post, similar to that which I proposed for you in the bank at Athens, and that might be vacant soon, in London. Since, to please my bride, (who is devoted to her mother), I intend to make my home in Paris, I have made arrangements for you to take that post now, if you will.

"'Shortly after this epistle a formal note will reach you, explaining all details. You will, I am sure, not refuse me the great pleasure of smoothing a little your path, under the present circumstances—since it is a very dear wish of mine to see you and Miss Sylvia happy.

"'I foresee no obstacles now to your wishes. Explain to Sir James that I intend to be your best friend, and shall be able, no doubt, to be of great assistance to you if you adopt this career.

"'At some future date I hope to present to you Mademoiselle de Beaugarde—and looking forward to your reply, I remain,

"'My dear Woodville,

"'Yours, with a thousand good wishes,

"'G. RIDOKANAKI.

"'P.S.—I should have written at greater length, but I am expecting Madame Beaugarde and her daughter, as I am to escort them to see some pictures. You will, therefore, grant me your indulgence for the bold, almost abrupt way in which I have conveyed to you my news. You will make excuses for the happy lover! She has an oval face, with a peach-like complexion. Her eyes resemble sapphires: her teeth are like pearls. Let me hear from you soon.'"

"Now, isn't he a wonderful chap?" asked Woodville. "And the best fellow in the world. I always liked him. How gifted he is! He describes people in detail, and by the yard, without giving one the very slightest idea of their appearance. He has a real genius for platitudes."

"And what an original description! Peach cheeks and sapphire eyes! Fruit and jewellery! But I daresay she's a dear, and I forgive him now. And Frank, *do* you realise what this means—to us?"

"I've been realising it since the first post this morning, Sylvia."

"You'll accept it?"

"Naturally. Everything is right, as you said it would be. We'll tell Sir James to-day."

"Look here, darling Frank, let me ring up a messenger to send a wire at *once* to accept, so that nothing can come between us!"

"Not just yet," said Woodville.

Savile's only comment when they told him was, "Just like that rotter to prefer another alien!" and he immediately wrote brief notes to Chetwode and Jasmyn Vere.

Sir James heard the news with real surprise and conventional indignation, principally because it was his practice to receive news in that way.

He refused his consent, sent Sylvia to her room, and turning round on Savile declared that the whole thing was caused by the disgraceful idleness of that boy, who ought to be at school. Such long holidays were not heard of in his younger days, and did the greatest harm mentally and physically to the boys and all their relatives.

The arrival of Aunt William diverted the storm. Sir James became far more angry with her for defending the young people than with them for requiring defence.

When she had left, he said that perhaps he would take it into consideration in a couple of years, if Woodville left the house at once, and they neither met nor corresponded in the interval.

At dinner he began to chaff them a little, and said Sylvia always got her own way with him.

After dinner, when he was smoking in the library, the desire to say "Take her, you dog, and be happy," or words to that effect, was too strong for him. He sent for Woodville, consented enthusiastically, and from that moment began to believe that with farseeing thoughtfulness he had planned her marriage from the very beginning. And he began to look forward to the list of political and other celebrities that would appear in the papers the day after the wedding.

Of course it was to be a long engagement and a quiet wedding; but entirely through the eager impetuosity of Sir James, they were married in six weeks, and every one said that in general splendour and gorgeousness it surpassed even the wedding of Sir James's elder daughter. Savile's attitude as best man was of such extraordinary correctness that it was the feature of the ceremony, and even distracted public attention from the bride and bridegroom.

THE END

Milton Keynes UK
Ingram Content Group UK Ltd.
UKHW042145281024
450365UK00010B/619